Matteo Carmignola

Partizipierte Offenbarung

Matteo Carmignola

Partizipierte Offenbarung

Ein Konzept zur biblischen Offenbarung im Vergleich zwischen Judentum und katholischem Lehramt

Fromm Verlag

Imprint

Cover image: www.ingimage.com

Publisher:
Fromm Verlag
is a trademark of
International Book Market Service Ltd., member of OmniScriptum Publishing Group
17 Meldrum Street, Beau Bassin 71504, Mauritius

Printed at: see last page
ISBN: 978-613-8-36075-9

Matteo Carmignola

Participatory Revelation

Ein Konzept zur biblischen Offenbarung im Vergleich zwischen Judentum und katholischem Lehramt

Abstract

Die Frage nach dem Schriftverständnis ist wesentlich von der Annahme bestimmt, inwiefern es sich um ein menschliches, also historisch-kulturelles Produkt handelt, oder ob es sich in seiner Gänze als Verschriftlichung der göttlichen Offenbarung beschreiben lässt. Der jüdische Theologe Benjamin Sommer geht dieser Thematik nach und diskutiert den Ansatz der *participatory revelation* um die Doppelnatur der Heiligen Schrift zu konzeptualisieren. Dabei werden exegetische, philosophische und theologiegeschichtliche Diskurse im Judentum und darüber hinaus rezipiert. Folgende Arbeit versucht Sommers Ansatz für das Judentum zu kontextualisieren und einen Vergleich zum katholischen Lehramt zu ziehen – dabei wird die dogmatische Konstitution Dei Verbum als Referenz herangezogen. In dieser Arbeit wird ersichtlich, wie das katholische Lehramt mit dem Diskurs der *participatory revelation* verknüpft werden und insbesondere von den exegetischen Arbeiten zum Alten Testament profitieren kann. Implikationen für die theologische Forschung und Pastoral werden im Anschluss der Synopse diskutiert.

Folgende Arbeit wurde als Diplomarbeit in englischer und deutscher Sprache an den Universitäten *Ben Gurion University of the Negev – Be'er Sheva (Israel)* und *Paris-Lodron Universität Salzburg* (Österreich) verfasst und zur Erlangung des akademischen Grades *Magister der Theologie (Mag. theol.)* an der *Theologisch-Katholischen Fakultät* vorgelegt und von *Univ.-Prof. Dr. Kristin De Troyer, BA. MA, Fachbereich Bibelwissenschaft und Kirchengeschichte* begutachtet.

The question concerning the nature of the Holy Scripture is mostly defined by the contrasting belief of it being a human artefact, or a recording of divine revelation. The Jewish theologian Benjamin Sommer discusses this issue using the concept of participatory revelation in order to express the ambiguity of authoritative religious scriptures. Notions from exegesis, philosophy, and history from a Jewish perspective and beyond are used to address this question. This thesis aims to contextualize Sommer's work within Judaism and to trace a comparison to Catholic doctrine. The dogmatic constitution Dei Verbum as the Catholic reference shows to be highly compatible with the discourse on participatory revelation. Catholic theology can profit from including exegetical expertise on the Old Testament to further develop its concept of revelation. Implications for theological research and pastoral care will be addressed following the synopsis.

Inhaltsverzeichnis

1 Dank

Das Verfassen einer Diplomarbeit leitet nicht nur den Abschluss eines Studiums ein, sondern ist in gewisser Weise auch ein Rückblick auf die fünf Jahre Universitätsleben und auf die unzähligen Ereignisse und Begegnungen, die damit verbunden sind. Dass diese fünf Jahre für mich zu einer so prägenden Zeit geworden sind, habe ich vielen Menschen zu verdanken, auch wenn ich sie hier alle nicht namentlich nennen kann. Dennoch möchte ich einige hervorheben, die gerade im Zusammenhang mit der Entstehung dieser Arbeit und dem Studienabschluss so wesentlich verbunden sind.

Per iniziare vorrei ringraziare i miei genitori che mi hanno sempre sostenuto in tutte le mie scelte formative e insieme ai miei fratelli hanno contribuito con il loro spirito critico a sviluppare un pensiero aperto e attento alle esigenze contemporanee.

Ganz wesentlich zur Findung des Themas der Arbeit und für den ersten Baustein haben meine Erasmus-Aufenthalte in Israel beigetragen, wofür ich ganz besonders Frau Ao.-Prof. Dr. Renate Egger-Wenzel danken möchte für die Initiative und die Begleitung der Studienaufenthalte in Haifa (2017) und Be'er Sheva (2018). For the period at the Ben-Gurion-University, I would like to express my gratitude to Dr. Atar Lineh for the warm welcome and the caring support during the months spent in Be'er Sheva and to Dr. Eran Viezel for the precious literature recommendations and the briefings on the topic from a Jewish perspective.

Für die Begleitung und Begutachtung der Arbeit möchte ich mich ganz herzlich bei Frau Univ.-Prof. Dr. Kristin De Troyer bedanken, die mir große Freiheit bei der Themenauswahl und beim Aufbau der Arbeit gewährte und mit wichtigen Hinweisen und Korrekturvorschlägen die Endgestalt mitprägte. Für das umsichtige und professionelle Lektorat der Arbeit möchte ich meine große Dankbarkeit gegenüber Frau Mag. Mira Obermayr ausdrücken, die sich insbesondere der sprachlichen Formulierungen der englischen Teile mit großer Sorgfalt angenommen hat.

2 Hinführung zur Arbeit

> Ein sehr dünner Mönch kommt mit einer aufgeschlagenen Bibel nach vorn, fanatisch den Finger auf einer Stelle stoßend: Was steht hier in der Schrift? »Sonne, steh still zu Gibeon und Mond im Tale Ajalon!« Wie kann die Sonne stillstehen, wenn sie sich nicht überhaupt dreht, wie diese Ketzer behaupten? Lügt die Schrift?[1]

So inszeniert Bertold Brecht in seinem Theaterstück *Leben des Galilei* nur eine der vielen Begegnungen, in denen die katholische Hierarchie die astronomischen Erkenntnisse zur Häresie erklärte – gerade aus Angst, dass ein Widerspruch zwischen den wissenschaftlichen Erkenntnissen und den Worten der Heiligen Schrift dem Wahrheitsgehalt der Bibel Abstriche machen könnten. Trotzt der formalen Rehabilitation von Galilei seitens der katholischen Kirche und auch einer Neuausrichtung, mit dem Verzicht, die Bibel als Dokument heranzuziehen, das versucht die „Einzelheiten der physischen Welt"[2] auszulegen, bleibt der Fall Galilei als Mythos einer, dem Fortschritt verschlossenen, Religion und einer unkritischen Verwendung der Heiligen Schrift erhalten. Der Blick auf die Gegenwart zeigt hingegen, wie – bis auf etwaiges Konfliktpotential mit KreationistInnen – die größten Diskrepanzen im Diskurs zwischen säkularen und religiösen Menschen sich gerade in sozialethischen Fragen finden lassen, insbesondere dort wo moralische Gebote aus Zitaten der Heiligen Schrift formuliert werden und diese – da sie Wort Gottes sind – als unfehlbar und nicht interpretierbar geltend gemacht werden.

Die Frage nach dem Verständnis von Schrift und, in Folge dessen, der Zugang zur Interpretation und wissenschaftlichen Exegese, ist wesentlich von der Annahme bestimmt, inwiefern es sich um ein menschliches, also historisch-kulturelles Produkt handelt, oder ob es sich in seiner Gänze als Verschriftlichung der göttlichen Offenbarung beschreiben lässt. Diese Annahmen stellen im Idealfall kein Entweder-Oder dar, sondern sollen gerade deshalb komplementär gedacht werden, da nur dadurch zum einen der Relevanz der biblischen Texte für die Glaubenspraxis Rechnung getragen werden kann und zugleich auch die Bibel als eine Sammlung von antiken Texten überhaupt Gegenstand von Auslegung und Forschung darstellt. Dieses komplementäre Verhältnis wird in pastoralen Schriften oft als *Gottes Wort in Menschen Wort* zum Ausdruck gebracht. Es war für mich daher umso spannender

[1] Brecht 2013, 60 dabei wird aus dem Buch Josua (10,12) zitiert

[2] Papst Johannes Paul II. 1992, Nr. 12

wissenschaftliche Konzepte zu finden, die diese doppelte Beschaffenheit von Heiliger Schrift systematisch behandeln und weitreichend beleuchten: Diesen Zugang habe ich in den Schriften des jüdischen Bibelwissenschaftlers, der am Jewish Theological Seminar (New York) lehrt, gefunden. In seinem Buch *Revelation and Authority*[3] beleuchtet er für das Judentum das Konzept einer partizipierten Offenbarung (participatory revelation) aus bibelwissenschaftlicher, philosophischer und religionshistorischer Sicht, welches gerade diese Doppelnatur von Schrift und Tradition in Hinblick auf göttlichen Ursprung und menschlicher Beteiligung zum Ausdruck bringen kann. Ziel dieser Arbeit ist es, das Werk von Sommer zu kontextualisieren und seinen Ansatz systematisch darzustellen, um dann mit dem katholischen Lehramt zu Offenbarung und Schrift Vergleiche zu ziehen. Im Anschluss sollen daraus entstehende Fragen diskutiert werden und Implikationen für die theologische Forschung wie für die schulische und pastorale Praxis herausgearbeitet werden. Teile dieser Arbeit, eben jene Kapitel zum Judentum, wurden auf Englisch verfasst, da sie zu wesentlichen Teilen an der Ben-Gurion-Universität in Be'er Sheva (Israel) entstanden sind. Die Sprache, der dort vorliegenden Literatur und mitunter auch die Möglichkeit, Teile von dort lehrenden ForscherInnen lesen zu lassen, hatten diese Entscheidung nahegelegt.

Zum Inhalt der Arbeit

Das Kapitel *Scripture – Some preliminary remarks* soll diese Diplomarbeit einleiten und aus einer religionswissenschaftlichen Perspektive herausarbeiten, welche Merkmale für Heilige Schriften in den Weltreligionen bestimmend sind. Themen der Autorität, des Einflusses und der Heiligkeit sowie der Einzigartigkeit der Schriften in religiösen Traditionen kommen im Einführungsteil zur Sprache und helfen die Darstellung des Forschungsthemas zu kontextualisieren. So etwa wird für die scheinbare Besonderheit des Judentums, wo zahlreiche nachbiblische Schriften die Bedeutung der Torah zur Debatte stellen, ersichtlich, wie dies keine Proprium der jüdischen Religion darstellt, sondern so auch in weiteren Weltreligionen zu finden ist. Das erste thematische Kapitel *Jewish Scripture(s) – An introduction* versucht anhand von drei Vorannahmen das wichtigste Wissen rund um das jüdische Schrifttum, dessen Stellenwert und die bibeltheologische Auseinandersetzung zu skizzieren. Erste Kontroversen, gerade um die Frage nach der Entstehung der biblischen Texte und der

[3] Sommer 2015

Relevanz und Autorität der verschiedene Korpora der Heiligen Schrift, werden dabei exemplarisch eingeleitet.

Das Hauptkapitel *Participatory Revelation in Judaism* soll das Thema zur Fragestellung dieser Arbeit ausführlich beleuchten. Dieser Teil ist gerade in Hinblick auf die Publikation von Benjamin Sommer verfasst worden, mit dem Versuch, seine Darstellung nachzuvollziehen und die kontextuellen Bezüge herzustellen, um den Vergleich mit der katholischen Theologie möglich zu machen. Dabei werden – nicht zuletzt aufgrund der Verankerung dieser Diplomarbeit im Fach der alttestamentliche Bibelwissenschaft – zuerst exegetische Betrachtungen herangezogen, welche aufzeigen, wie ein Konzept einer partizipierten Offenbarung kein rein philosophisches oder systematisch-spekulatives Unterfangen darstellt, sondern sich gerade aus der philologischen Arbeit an der Sinai Perikope (Ex 19-24) erschließen lässt. Hinführend dann zur systematischen Arbeit von Sommer werden drei jüdische Denker vorgestellt, welche die jüdische Philosophie der Moderne wesentlich prägten und über die religionsgemeinschaftlichen Grenzen hinweg auch das Verständnis von Bibel mitformten. Durch die Anführung von drei zentralen Thesen von B. Sommer soll seine Darstellung der *Participatory Revelation* für das Judentum umrissen werden, gerade in Hinblick der Bedeutung, was menschliche Beteiligung am religiös autoritativen Text darstellen kann.

Im dritten Teil der Arbeit soll der Transfer zur christlich-katholischen Auffassung von Bibel und Offenbarung hergestellt werden. Es werden in einer pointierten Übersicht kurz die Hauptthesen der dogmatischen Konstitution *Dei Verbum* aufgestellt, aus der hervorgehen, wie etliche Grundmotive eines partizipierten Offenbarungsverständnisses im Zweiten Vatikanischen Konzil schon verankert worden sind. Bedingungen und Möglichkeiten der Vergleichbarkeit des jüdischen und katholischen Konzeptes von *Participatory Revelation* sowie weitere Implikationen für die theologische und pastorale Arbeit mit den biblischen Schriften sollen im Diskussionsteil ausführlich aufgearbeitet werden.

3 Scripture – Some preliminary remarks

This introductory chapter aims to contextualize the study regarding the aspects of origin, authority and relevance of religious scriptures and to widen the focus on more general notions from perspective of comparative religious studies. These insights help to understand how some aspects, which would have been thought to be a characteristic of a certain denomination, are also common for other religions. In addition, through undertaking this approach, also factors outside the mere text, such as the liturgical and pedagogical use, are considered when researching biblical texts.

In German-speaking countries, probably every child who attended school classes on religious education might have learned that Judaism, Christianity, and Islam are *"Buchreligionen"* where faith and cult are based on a book, which is venerated as holy. Before preoccupying myself with this topic, I did not know that this term does not merely describe a popular scientific concept brought up by religious educators but that it is also an academic terminology coined by Siegfried Morenz.[4] As an Egyptologist and historian of religion, he also delivered general philosophical considerations on religions, like his highly-quoted distinction between *book religion* and *cult religion.*

Morenz's reflections refer to the Mediterranean area and his comparison between book and cult religion contraposes the three Abrahamitic traditions to which he contrasts pagan cults (Greek, Roman, and Egyptian). Even if his categorical way to present his observations might appear exaggerated and biased from a historical and ethnological perspective, he also delivers some far-reaching insights: First, book *and* cult religions both offer holy writings, but these differ in their function. For the cult religions, he defines its function as *serving* since the writings provide instructions and formulas for rituals. The final aim of cult religions is the representation of the divine myth. Book religions, on the other side, do not conceive their writing as a mean to a secondary purpose. The starting point and the final aim lay in the book itself. For this, the concern to preserve the integrity of the exact wording is a characteristic of book religions.[5] Secondly, we might also consider Morenz's notion on the distinction between seeing and hearing. For the people of Israel, he identifies the importance of hearing since it granted an extraordinary status to this nation. Many biblical narratives

4 Morenz 1950

5 Morenz 1950, 711

prove this, where God speaks to and trough his prophets while it is not possible to see him; however, this invisibility also bestows fear.[6]

On the other hand, cult religions (Hellenism and Roman) lay focus on the visual perception as they seek to see God's gestalt, his epiphany. Therefore, statues are created in order to bundle their veneration. Thus, a contrast can be drawn to the Israel's *importance of hearing,* where the scripture is so central as God's words are only present to those who hear them.

To further extend this first introduction on what scripture is and which functions it obtains in religious traditions, I will use some remarks by William Graham[7], who offers a general criteriology for characteristical attributes of scripture. Three of them should be reported to outline what the elements, functions, and characteristics of Holy Writings consist of.

3.1 Power

Texts, which are acknowledged to be a scripture, exert a noticeable influence on human life. The words not only carry a semantical meaning but have a performative character as well: "For the faithful, a sacred word is not merely a word, but an operative, salvific word."[8] Graham traces this power back to the source of words and the analogy, which is created with the narratives of the cosmogonies; not only the Judaeo-Christian tradition recognizes the creation of the world as a result of the speech of God. Several religious cults, Egyptian, Quranic, or African mythologies, regard the creation as the result of God's speech.[9] Like in Genesis 1:3 וַיֹּאמֶר אֱלֹהִים יְהִי אוֹר וַיְהִי־אוֹר׃ where the root of the first verb אמר means *utter, say*. If nature obeys the speech of God, his word will also wield its power on the faithful readers through the scriptures containing it.

One example of the inherent and latent power might be found in the Rabbinic principle "all holy scriptures defile the hands."[10] This perplexing and ambiguous

---

[6] Morenz 1950, 714 refers here to several biblical quotation as: Ex 20:20, So Moses went up and the Lord said to him, "Go down and warn the people so they do not force their way through to see the Lord and many of them perish." or 24:27 To the Israelites the glory of the Lord looked like a consuming fire on top of the mountain.

[7] Graham 1987

[8] Graham 1987, 140

[9] Graham 1987, 141

[10] Lim 2010, 501

expression from Mishnah Yadayim 3:5 seems to contradict the concept of holiness of scripture as for how it could cause impurity.[11] Before diving more into detail of the research done on the origins of the mentioned Mishnah principle, a diametrical opposite phrase from a Catholic tradition might exemplify the power dimension of scripture: According to the English Mass Order, after the proclamation from the Gospel, following instruction is given:

> Then he kisses the book, saying quietly:
> Through the words of the Gospel may our sins be wiped away.[12]

In a Canadian parish, I experienced it done very expressively by saying it out loud to the assembly and, with a generous hand gesture reaching from the book to the community, the priest seemed to pass out the blessing coming from the book. The recollection of this memory occurred through Graham's observations on worship of the power of scripture:

> In most scriptural traditions, such perceived power manifests itself within both 'orthoprax' and 'popular' spirituality in tendencies towards bibliolatry – the treatment of scripture as an object of worship or as a locus of supernatural power.[13]

In this specific case, I see the lines between bibliolatry and locus of supernatural power blurred.

Likewise, a notion of supernatural power exists as well in the Rabbinic "enigma" of the Holy Scripture defiling the hands. Timothy H. Lim[14] reports several attempts done by scholars to find the correct interpretation of what this Rabbinic principle might really mean. To his judgment, the right approach is to look into the narrative of the Ark of the Covenant. For the Israelis leaving the Exile of Egypt, the Ark was the holiest, most precious, and sacred object since it was a testimony of God's presence. Through the Books of Samuel, we know that the Ark was not only a blessing for Israel but also a lethal power for its enemies and those unworthy to touch: 1 Sam 5 reports how the Philistines in Ashod had been punished with tumors for stealing the Ark and as a guilt offering, besides having to return the Ark, they had to submit golden figures

[11] Lim 2010

[12] International Committee on English in the Liturgy 2010, 9

[13] Graham 1987, 141

[14] Lim 2010

of the tumor and the mice that ravaged the land (1 Sam 6:4). However, even the ones with the intention to save the Ark got punished with death:

> When they came to the threshing floor of Nakon, Uzzah reached out and took hold of the ark of God, because the oxen stumbled. The Lord's anger burned against Uzzah because of his irreverent act; therefore God struck him down, and he died there beside the ark of God. (2 Sam 6:6-7)

This narrative of the Ark, containing the Covenant of God, was transposed to the Holy Writings since they contained the Name of God in the Tetragrammaton[15]. This made them too sacred to be touched by lay people or outside a sacred wall:

> Only the priest is eligible to handle holy scriptures, maybe within the Temple. For all others, holy scriptures make hands but the whole person ritually defiled as a means of protecting the sacred writings from misuse.[16]

Through studying these examples, we can identify how scriptures exert power on their believers. It constitutes social and moral order and assigns roles and functions to the population (priest and lay) by determining or influencing the moral status (e.g. sinful, clean, unclean).

3.2 Authority and Sacrality

The most prominent evidence for the authority of holy writings is the fact that scriptures contain texts of legal nature. These laws discipline the communal life and, in particular, the cultic and religious order of the community of believers; furthermore, some would be used for sanctioning of criminal acts. Even if in some cases an explanation is given for the meaning and the reason behind a prohibition or commandment, the status of authority of the scripture is by itself the last rational given for the question why to obey to the given verdict. According to Graham, the fact that scripture "provides the legal basis of communal order [...] is most evident" in the Islamic tradition where the Quran is the basis for the shari'a and, of course, in Jewish scripture as well.[17] Even if Sweeney remarks that to narrow down "Torah" to the

[15] Actually, not all writings from the Hebrew Bible contain the Tetragrammaton. Disputes in Rabbinic literature commenting on the Mishnah Yadayim 3:5 argued whether the defilement of the hands occurs as well for the Book of Esther, Qohelet, and the Song of Songs. e. g. Lim 2010, 501-504

[16] Lim 2010, 513

[17] Graham 1987, 141

meaning of "Law" is not accurate,[18] the wide extent of legal texts in Jewish scripture cannot be denied. While some Christian textbooks on the Old Testament identify parts of it as legal elements – mainly the three bodies of law from the Pentateuch[19]–, the classification of what is a legal text is much broader from a Jewish point of view. As Barton[20] states, even a m*inimalist approach* would include *narratives dealing with legal issue* (e. g. Salomon's ruling in 1 Kings 3:16-28) as well as the collection of laws composed by the *prophet Ezekie*l (Ez 40-48) for the category of legal text, along with the laws from the Pentateuch. In addition, the maximalist approach sees all "texts from biblical narratives, prophecy, and the wisdom literature that mention or allude to the laws of the Pentateuch"[21] as part of legal texts as well.

This is to show, how considerable attention is paid to any element from scripture which might be understood as a binding instruction. Thus, the field for commentaries and legal interpretations is open to discussion if and how an assertation from scripture has to be followed by the faithful community in contemporary life. How coherent and accurate the legalistic reception and application are executed cannot be stated in general. However, a quite cynical remark from Jacob Neusner gets to the heart of this issue:

> So the role of Scripture in the communities of Judaism is to validate what people want to say anyway. The place of Scripture can be described pretty much in terms of opposites: paramount and subordinated, definitive and wholly secondary, source of truth and font of proof texts and pretexts.[22]

The visual, sensorial counterpart of authority is the characteristic element of sacrality. While the first characteristic is shown in legal disputes and tractates, the sacrality manifests itself in art and liturgy. Several religious traditions express their reverence for the holiness of its scripture by decorating and enshrining it. Graham[23] indicates how in Islam calligraphy is a way to express the beauty and sacrality of the

---

[18] Sweeney 2008, 197 even speaks of a mistranslation opting for a meaning as "instruction", "guidance", or "revelation"

[19] Zenger 2008, 83 elencates the Book of Convenant [Bundesbuch] Ex 20:22-23:33, the Laws of Holiness [Heiligkeitsgesetz] Lev 17-26, and the Deuteronomistic Laws [Deuteronomistische Gesetzessammlung] Dtn 12-26.

[20] Barton 2016, 160

[21] Barton 2016, 160

[22] Neusner 1982, 64

[23] Graham 1987, 141

message of the Qur'an as well as the embroidery of the covers for the Torah scrolls in Judaism, along with its special shrine, the Torah ark in Synagogue. Similar expressions of reverence can also be found in Buddhism and Sikh worship. Moreover, ritual gestures as the elevation of the Book of Gospels in Catholic liturgy or the procession of the Torah with touching and kissing of its cover also display the veneration of the sacrality of scripture.

Indeed, liturgy represents a crucial point when discussing authority. In the observation of rituals, we can obtain first hints regarding the question if and how a hierarchical distinction is made between the components of scriptural texts. Why has the Torah a very ostensible shrine while the Megillot are kept in a less decorated cabin? Why, in Catholic service, is the Gospel introduced by chants and venerated with incense on festivities while the other readings are not? For the particular question if there is a hierarchy between the texts of the Hebrew canon, a section in the next chapter will follow.

For this general introduction, we might observe that a distinction within scriptural textes accompanied by a hierarchy between the writings is common to many relgions. Graham refers to it as "more than one level of or degree of sacred texts in community"[24]. We can find this in Islam with the Qur'an vs. the Hadith as well as in Hinduism with the Veda vs. the Puranas. In addition, even if an ontological supremacy of the most sacred book or section of the book is stated, semi-scriptural books might still take a more visible role in religious life and personal piety. This aspect will be discussed in detail through Jewish scriptures with the question of the status of the Rabbinic literature.

The authority and sacrality of scriptures are also connected with the practice of *pseudepigraphy* and *pseudonymity*. Both practices stand for the creation of new texts by imitating and emulating canonical scriptures and or by publishing them under the name of a venerated person to achieve higher reception in religious communities.[25] What seems like fraud to the ear of modern readers was a widely spread custom in antiquity, which was also driven by noble intents. Silverman[26] reports two classical explanations why such practices are so common in Jewish and Christian scriptures:

[24] Graham 1987, 142

[25] More in detail see van der Toorn 2009, 33–39

[26] Silverman 2011

One argument (the so-called "traditional perspective") states that the writer of the text held a narrative or a religious message that had only been passed on orally. Since he or she does not identify himself/herself as the author but the authorship is located in the continuity of the tradition he/she opts to divulge the texts under a name which stands for the legacy of the (religious) tradition. The other explanation (the so-called "school" view) is derived from the study of epigraphy as a general Greco-Roman phenomenon, where "the author writes in the persona of, the spirit of, and honor of his master as a way of continuing his memory and work. As the traditional view, the actual author considers himself unimportant to the meaning or content of the work."[27] To sum up, literary phenomena as pseudoepigraphy (and pseudonymity) stand for the authority already attributed to a specific collection of texts and occur in a period when the process of Canon formation is ongoing or terminated.[28]

3.3 Unicity

As the third category from a selection of Graham's remarks on scripture, the topic of unicity in the sense of "unicity of source, content, and authority"[29] should be discussed. As we compare the characteristics of scriptures across religious tradition, we see how only some of the texts are believed to be composed by a single writer (e.g. the Qur'an by the Prophet Muhammad, or the Book of Mormon), while several other denominations recognise a scripture as a collection of texts. Despite the noticeable diversity of the content and genre of the texts (narrations, collections of laws, letters, lyrics, etc.), the collection, which composes the scripture, is conceived as a unity, "both in its ontological origin, authoritativeness and internal consistency as sacred truth."[30]

Since scriptural texts are believed to be of divine origin, it is coherent to emphasize commonalities and to see differences as secondary. But still, if we just consider the five books of the Torah, we find an internal diversity and a partially controversial plurality, which can be read as different theologies forging the message.

---

[27] Silverman 2011, 523

[28] See Meade 1986, 199 for Christian pseudonymity. He introduces the concept of 'Canon-consciousness' "to designate the growing awareness on the part of the authors and their communities of the authoritative nature of the traditions they were handling, and the increasingly rigid form that those traditions took in both content and literary expression"

[29] Graham 1987, 141

[30] Graham 1987, 141

To study the plurality between and within the texts of the Pentateuch, biblical science is engaged in the research program of the *Documentary Hypothesis* since the 18th century, where a differentiation of four sources (the Jahvist, Elohist, Deuteronomy, and Priestly), three redactors, and three stages[31] provide a model to explain plurality as a result of developments of and inside the texts. Plurality between the texts is the result of what is called the canon formation. How a canon, the list of those texts which have the status of authoritative scripture, is formed cannot be answered reliably, even though serious academic research has been done on the Christian[32] and Hebrew Bible Canon[33]. For the Hebrew Bible, contemporary scholars reject the idea of it having been the product of theological criteria (what Christians would identify as a Synod or Council) but develop rather practice-based models by which the canon was gradually formed[34]. Thus, state-of-the-art biblical scholar work confirms what a historian of religion stated in general:

> Nowhere in history of religion has the process of canon formation been a clear or unequivocal one [...] In most cases, it is finally not the fiat of a council or individual religious authority seeking to force a canon in order to delimit orthodoxy, but rather the usage of the majority that determinates any canon of the sacred and authority scripture.[35]

Even so, the focus on the differences is a merely academic and scholar endeavor while the religious practice ignores these discrepancies or harmonizes them. Also from a theological standpoint, Barr argues that "the locus of 'unity' lies in the regulative decisions that, though arising in part from the Bible, become the interpretative guide for religion afterwards."[36] As a result, it can be concluded that also the characteristics of unity are a (post-hoc) cultivated element produced by a group of believers rather than an inherent property of the texts themselves.

[31] Kratz 2011, XI

[32] Metzger 1997

[33] Lim 2013

[34] Van der Toorn 2009, 233–47

[35] Graham 1987, 142

[36] Barr 2004, 153

4 *Jewish* Scripture(s) – An introduction

To understand the extend and the dynamic of religious scriptures in Judaism, this chapter introduces the distinction of Written and Oral Torah and briefly touches upon the history and development of the postbiblical writings. Furthermore, the relevence of the corpora and its complementarity is adressed in the discussion of a commonly held concept where Christian readers might expect to see a primacy of the Written over the Oral Torah while Jewish life would suggest otherwise. To further contextualize the work on participatory revelation, a brief overview on the aims and particularities of biblical theology is given.

One thing that the first encounter with Judaism taught me is an alternative approach to a systematic analysis. If we read Maimonides, or a paragraph from rabbinic literature, or at times even contemporary scholarly literature, we see how a more narrative, story-telling approach is chosen over an analytical argumentation. Therefore, I would also like to start with the reflection of some commonly held concepts regarding Judaism and Jewish scriptures. As a young scholar educated in Catholic theology in a German-speaking environment, I experienced several aha-moments while reading the first introductory chapters of books on Jewish biblical studies. These eye-openers were either determined by the obvious differences to Christian concepts on scriptures and religion, or by the surprising commonalities between Jewish thought and Catholic theology, which, in return, differ from theological concepts of reformed Christian denominations.

These three commonly held concepts should serve as subchapters to offer a summary of what might be essential knowledge in order to write and read a thesis on a specific topic on Jewish and Christian concepts of biblical revelation.

4.1 Is the (Hebrew) Bible *one* Book?

The first visual association with the word "Bible" might be that of a hardcover book with very thin pages. This assumption does not surprise since the Bible is worldwide the most widely distributed and most translated book in history.[37] But, still speaking of the Christian bible, a first look into the etymology of this term shows how the Greek word τὰ βιβλία is indicating a plural; the term stands for a collection of books rather than a monograph. However, the discussion on the Christian canon, how it was formed, and how it changes between the denominations will be omitted in this paper since it can be found in almost every introductory textbook on the Christian

[37]http://www.guinnessworldrecords.com/world-records/best-selling-book-of-non-fiction/ [25.01.2017]

bible. The essential point is that – beyond the insight that the Bible, Christian or Hebrew, is not *a* book but a *collection of books* – the 24 books from the Hebrew Bible do not fully cover what is relevant as Holy Scriptures for Rabbinic Judaism. Therefore, according to Benjamin Sommer, whatever might be called Jewish biblical theology cannot be chiefly biblical and only comprehend the 24 books of the Tenak: it "must [be based] on Judaism's rich post-biblical tradition at least as much as on scripture."[38]

So, what else should be considered if we discuss scripture including the Jewish perspective? Most Christians, including myself prior to studying this topic more closely, ignore that post-biblical writings as the Talmud are also called Torah. In fact, even in scholarly literature, a reader encounters a confusing and sometimes frustrating equivocal usage of the term "Torah". Torah might indicate a book or all the five books of the Pentateuch, the whole Tanak as well as authoritative Rabbinic writings. In some cases, the author explicates at the beginning of his thesis, how he or she will use the term and the reader has to hope that he or she will be loyal to his/her plan.

For non-Jewish readers, an introduction on which books are authoritative in Judaism and how they are related might be necessary. With the help of Steven Fraade[39], I will try to deliver a brief systematic overview before we delve into the single sections:

First, we can distinguish between *Written Torah* and *Oral Torah*. Written Torah is the collection of 24 Books that represent the Hebrew Bible, which is divided into three sections: the Torah (5 Books), the Prophets – נְבִיאִים [nebi'im] – (4 Former Prophets, 3+1 Latter Prophets), and the Writings – כְּתוּבִים [ketubi'im] (11 Books). Put together from the initials of each section, the word Tanak [also used: TaNaK, Teanach, Tanek, Tanakh] indicates the canon of the biblical writings. On the other hand, the Oral Torah is a multi-layered concept: it refers also to writings, but the notion "oral" indicates that the content of these books has been passed down orally for a longer period than the material which became the Written Torah. Therefore, the Hebrew terms מקרא [miqra, that which is read], and Midrash [midrash, repeating] illustrate this first distinction between Written and Oral Torah quite well.

On the level of the Oral Torah, we find several tractates and collections of writings, which pick up biblical passages, comment on them and/or add other

[38] Sommer 2009, 1
[39] Fraade 2012, 32

elements. These elements are not passed down in the biblical writings but they are still authoritative since they too are traced back to the revelation at Sinai.[40] In general, two types of oral tradition are defined: (1) The *Midrash* (מדרש stands for seeking of meaning, expression) presenting various commentaries on passages of the Hebrew Bible. A Midrash could contain part of the Halakah (הֲלָכָה the way to go) with legal and legalistic considerations or part of the Aggadah (from the Aramaic אַגָּדָה tale, narration) with a more narrative approach. (2) The *Mishnah* (מִשְׁנָה study [by repetition]) contains grouped lists of Rabbinic laws, which, in some cases, have some or minimal references to biblical sources.[41]

Some of the components, which, for the most part, have been handed down orally in the 3rd century CE, were written down by Rabbis in commented editions.[42] These tractates are known as Talmud (תַּלְמוּד teaching, instruction) for which two versions exist: the Jerusalem (Palestinian) Talmud and the Babylonian Talmud. Concerning the dating of the final composition, the indications are quite vague with a range from the third to the fifth century C.E. for the Jerusalem Talmud[43] and seventh century for the Babylonian Talmud.[44]

For a more accurate discussion, each of the mentioned elements should be briefly introduced and contextualized in its development:

Midrash stands for Rabbinic commentaries on biblical texts. The Hebrew root דרש – seeking, searching – coins this term, which can be interpreted as the search for meaning, an explanation, teaching in the Torah. For this, Midrash as an activity has also been practiced in biblical times, as some references in chronicles or in the Book of Ezra might indicate.[45] The term Midrash itself, primarily, does not indicate a distinct book, even if several anthologies of Midrashim have existed from the 11th century onwards.[46] It rather stands for an exegetical approach to biblical sentences and

[40] Chapter 3.3.3 discusses this in detail and necessary depth. At this point we might already introduce the concept of Dual Torah since it is the basis for the authority of postbiblical writings in Rabbinic Judaism: "The Dual Torah refers to a corpus of rules, orally formulated and orally handed on, impsissima verba of God to Moses at Sinai." Neusner 2005, 1708

[41] This overview is based on Fraade 2012, 32

[42] Stemberger 1992, 41–45

[43] Jewish Encyclopedia [06.02.2017]; Neusner 2001, XXXII

[44] Neusner 2002, 220

[45] Wigoder, Skolnik and Himelstein 2002, 528 indicate how in Ezra 7:10 a first distinction and interdependence between Written and Oral Torah is alluded

[46] Wigoder, Skolnik and Himelstein 2002, 533–35

narratives. According to the methodology and the content of the Midrashim, a distinction is made between *Midrash Aggadah* for the narrative, to some extent also allegorical and storied, and the *Midrash Halakhah* for the legal work. Both have in common the search for an additional, more concrete and illustrative meaning to the words of the biblical texts.

The *Aggadah* could be described as "fragments of sermons delivered in the synagogue on Friday evenings or Shabbat afternoons."[47] The biblical text is taken to answer questions arising from the religious life with its daily problems and concerns. For this – and this might be too different from what is often done in pastoral care in modern times – the text is interpreted freely with the consequence of

> a meaning diametrically opposed to its original intent. Thus, for example, the first verse of Lamentations ("Jerusalem has become like a widow") is turned into an expression of optimistic hope: "Like a widow, but not actually a widow. Rather as a woman whose husband has gone abroad but who intends to return to her" (MK 20a).[48]

Midrash Aggadah harmonizes a passage, which possibly did sound harsh to the community or an allegorical meaning can be read between the lines in order to deliver a social message. These are just of the common approaches used in Midrash literature. Carl Bakhos lists several more:

> expansive paraphrase, filling in scriptural gaps; contractive paraphrase, removing discomforting sections or details; relocating laws or narratives to more congenial settings; harmonizing seemingly discordant verses; narrativizing laws and legalizing narratives; calendarizing biblical laws and narratives; identifying anonymous with named persons and places; etiologizing later practices or beliefs; and the list could go on.[49]

Midrash Halakah, on the other side, is an exposition written to clarify legal issues. It is meant to identify and make explicit which commandments and laws can be found in the Written Torah, in particular the Books Leviticus and Numeri, and how these laws are to be followed by Jews. In addition, further laws are contained, which are believed to also have been given to Moses at the Mount Sinai but having been passed on only orally since they are not contained in the Five Books. Above that, later commandments, like the procedures of the Shabbat or the instructions for festivities

[47] Wigoder, Skolnik and Himelstein 2002, 533

[48] Wigoder, Skolnik and Himelstein 2002, 528

[49] Bakhos 2006, 62

like Purim, are contained in the Halakah as well, which are clearly from a post-biblical Rabbinic origin.[50]

The misdrashic Halakah is attributed to sages, which are called Soferim (סוֹפְרִים; scribes, counter). In the Second Temple period (~450 BCE), they set the foundations for the Oral Torah: "They taught the halakhot and the traditions in close connection with the study of the Bible and deduced new halakhot through the interpretation of the written text."[51] Also in this case, Halakah *per se* does not indicate a tractate or a book but rather the exegetical method of "the expounding of the text in order to substantiate halakhic rulings".[52] Similar to for the Aggadah, the explanatory clarifications of the Halakah often go beyond the biblical text. They reach a momentum where Rabbinic exegesis formulates Halakha ruling without poor or any reference to the biblical text. But, in order to "rescue" the Halakah from Christian anti-law sentiments, we might consider some notions of Jacob Neusner on how the Halakah became so central for the Jewish identity and is a main source of theological and anthropological consideration. Contrary to Christian apologetics, which sees law as opposit to faith[53], Neusner insistently emphasizes on how Halakha focuses on the Jewish inner life and on the interiority of the relationships:

> The Halakhah embodies the extension of God's design for world order into the inner-facing relationships of (1) God and Israel (2) Israel's inner order in its own terms, and (3) the Israelite's household viewed on its own in time and space and social circumstance.[54]

To sum up, *Midrash* is a generic term of "sprawling" biblical exegesis and commentaries looking for a narrative (Aggadah) or legal (Halakah) meaning behind the text. It has its beginning in the time of the Second Temple period – as the Books of Ezra and Nehemiah indicate – and has been transmitted orally for the most part. From the 13th century onwards, known editions have been published, like the *Midrash Ha-Gadol* in the middle ages, which have been re-edited in the 20th century by Solomon Schechter and other Jewish scholars.[55]

---

[50] Wigoder, Skolnik and Himelstein 2002, 323

[51] Encyclopaedia Judaica 2007

[52] Wigoder, Skolnik and Himelstein 2002, 323

[53] I will discuss this in Chapter 2.3

[54] Neusner 2001, xxxviii

[55] Encyclopaedia Judaica 1971b

The *Mishnah*, on the other side, constitutes the first authoritative assembling of the Oral Torah. It is also composed by narrative and legal traditions, but the legal elements, the Halakhah, prevail.[56] The collection of the Mishnah looks back to decades and centuries of Rabbinic disputes, as "nearly 150 different sages are named in the Misnah."[57] The redactor is the venerated Rabbi *Yehudah ha-Nasi,* who lived in the Western Galilee in the 3rd century CE.[58] The Mishnah is composed of six tractates, sometimes ordered by topic and sometimes arranged by the Rabbi or sage whose observations are reported. In scholarship, the question if the Mishnah was intended as a legal code or as an educational tool is still at the centre of some disputes:

> Some recent scholars suggest that Mishnaic forms and principles reflect the conceptual foundations of the Mishnah's halakhic thinking. The frequent aggadic pronouncements and anecdotes within the Misnah, which are interwoven with the halakhic material in a highly sophisticated literary manner, may be seen as supporting this last viewpoint [the educational hypothesis].[59]

The Mishnah is followed by more written Rabbinic literature with the function to propose additional insides and comment on passages from the Mishnah and Midrash. The *Tosefta*, which is dated around 300 CE[60], is considered to be the first commentary on the Mishnah "explaining or expanding upon laconic Mishnah formulations"[61] with additional production of new text segments.[62] Some scholars also think of the Tosefta as a product of the original Mishnah redaction, which then had to be edited as an additional text after the redaction of the Mishnah was concluded.[63]

Parallel to finishing the Mishnah and its wide distribution among the Jewish world, a further stage of commenting was carried out. From the 2nd century onwards – after the destruction of the Second Temple and the Jewish wars – many Jews were living in the diaspora and this contributed to a more advanced process of collecting and commenting on traditional collection of the Mishnah:

[56] Wigoder, Skolnik and Himelstein 2002, 540

[57] Wigoder, Skolnik and Himelstein 2002, 541

[58] Stemberger 1992, 138

[59] Walfish 1997a, 472

[60] Neusner 2001, XXXII

[61] Walfish 1997b, 700

[62] Stemberger 1992, 161–62

[63] Walfish 1997b, 700

> Indeed, the publication and the subsequent wide circulation of the Mishnah changed the way the Oral Law was studied. Instead of formulating new *mishnayyot* (laws from the Mishnah) the rabbis, beginning with the colleagues and students of R. Judah ha-Nasi, now began to analyze the Mishnah. [64]

Two terms are used to describe this process and its product as writing: *Gemara* and *Talamud.* Gemara is an Aramaic word (גְּמָרָא; lit. "completion" or "tradition")[65] which stands for discussion and elaborations of Rabbis on the text and passages of the Mishnah. Since the Talmud reports on passages of the Gemara combining it with the reference text from the Mishnah, the term Gemare was often used – as *pars pro toto* – for the entire Talmud. The *Talmud* can be considered as the most extensive and most authoritative collection of the Oral Law. The term תַּלְמוּד means "teaching" and is applied to the vast collections of comments from authoritative Jewish scholars from 200-500CE, the so-called "classic period of rabbinic Judaism".[66] Two Talmuds are known, the *Talmud Yerushalmi* (Jerusalem Talmud) and the *Talmud Bavli* (Babylonian Talmud), which stand for the geographic region of the Rabbinic academies studying the Oral Torah. Even though the Talmud is 90% "a systematic exegesis of the Mishnah and amplification of its laws"[67], the range of topics and wisdom collected in these volumes is astonishing:

> The Talmud has correctly been described as dealing with religion and ethics, exegesis and homiletics, jurisprudence and ceremonial law, ritual and liturgy, philosophy and science, medicine and magic, astronomy and astrology, history and geography, commerce and trade, politics and social problems. Thus the Talmud serves as prime source material for knowledge of the real and intellectual world of late antiquity in general, and of classical Jewish law and doctrine in particular.[68]

From 425 CE on, first editions of the Talmud began to circulate[69] and in the centuries following its publication an incessant study and scholar commentary on it took place. Each era brought its most famous commentaries, from the medieval ages with Rashi and Maimonides, to the enlightenment and also in modern times a critical-historical approach to Talmud studies can be found.

---

[64] Wigoder, Skolnik and Himelstein 2002, 747

[65] Encyclopaedia Judaica 1971a

[66] Friedmann and Moscovitz 1997, 668

[67] Neusner 2002, 143

[68] Friedmann and Moscovitz 1997, 669

[69] Wigoder and Werblowsky 1997, 748

4.2 Is there a distinctive primacy of the Written Torah?

The second preconception of a Christian mind might be the assumption that if there were several more authoritative writings besides the Bible that at least the books of the Bible would be superordinate to post-biblical Rabbinical writings. This is the case for liturgy where the reading and the veneration of the Written Torah is central to the weekly service, but for matters of the organization of the religious life, the Oral Torah is more relevant: We can observe this in regard to dietary laws, for the ritual objects, the calendar of festivities, and for many other central components of Jewish religion. This shift of relevance is also common in Christian traditions, as the biblical books are less relevant for the organization of the Catholic faith-life while references to the Catechism and the church doctrine are needed to explain many practices of the religious life. Nevertheless, in Judaism, the extent of this shift of relevance reaches further to what even the Catholic church practises: Greenspahn[70] speaks of a "Jewish ambivalence towards the bible" where, in several perspectives, in former and in contemporary times, the Tenakh is secondary to the Rabbinic writings. Three aspects will be considered: education and curriculum, the nature of the Rabbinic writings, and also Christian hostilities causing this ambivalence.

Alone according to the etymology of the term, we can consider the Talmud as an educational curriculum covering all essential areas of knowledge. Indeed, even the instruction to study the Torah is taken from the Mishnah and the Talmud, with the indication that the study of the Torah begins at age 5.[71] Keeping in mind the ambivalent usage of Torah, we might consider Holtz's notion[72] on how the instruction of the Talmud cannot be read as incitement to study the entire Bible, but rather the books which are heavily discussed in the Rabbinic writings. Traditionally and to some extent until today, Jewish education starts with the Book of Leviticus and the matters of ritual impurity and animal offering.[73] Holtz describes how most of the Jewish education regarding the Bible is done through the Rabbinic lens by a selection of liturgically and

[70] Greenspahn 2007

[71] Holtz 2011, 373–74 refers here to the Mishnah Avot (5:21) and the Talmud Bavli Batra 21a, also indicating how the passage from the Mishnah is a medieval addition.

[72] Holtz 2011, 374

[73] Myjewishlearning.com 2018

ritually relevant passages and in a traditional understanding given by Rabbinic interpretation.[74]

In contemporary Israeli society, a non-Rabbinic Bible study is seen as a secular endeavor and is taught as a non-religious subject in the school curriculum. It is deeply connected with Zionist aspirations, which purposely choose the Tanakh over the Rabbinic writings and read the Hebrew Bible without religious guidance.[75] But even in Jewish academic studies, the status of biblical studies was not seen as genuine Jewish but considered as inferior – also regarding intellectual demand and academic prestige – to Talmud studies.[76]

The question concerning the curriculum, whether the Written or the Oral Torah should be studied first and more intensively, is deeply intertwined with the nature of the Rabbinic post-biblical writings themselves. First, we have to consider, how in Rabbinic Judaism both, the Oral and the Written Torah, have been revealed by God to Moses at Sinai. In Chapter 3.3.3 we will deal with this subject in depth. Secondly, the Oral Torah, as an exegesis on passages from the Tanakh, can be considered an anthology of the most relevant passages, laws and narratives from the Written Torah plus a correct understanding and further comandments given in the revelation at Sinai[77]. Therefore, the Rabbinic oral tradition can cover more than the 24 Books of the written Hebrew Bible. It might not come as a surprise how many disputes on the prevalence were solved by a very pragmatic argument, as Sommer summarizes one moderated position on the curriculum dispute:

> There is an agreement in principle that ideally, a Jew should study both Written Torah (in particular the Pentateuch) and Oral Torah, but some authorities maintain that one can fulfil this dual obligation by studying Oral Torah alone, after all, rabbinic literature quotes scripture quite often, so by studying the rabbis one kills two birds with one stone.[78]

[74] Holtz 2011, 375 *However, we must consider how the study of traditional Rabbinic exegesis is not merely a passive memorization of one authoritative opinion but rather an engaged dispute confronting several authoritative opinions on a Biblical section. In the same volume,* Lehman and Kanarek 2011, 583 *explain how studying the Talmud still matters as contemporary teaching model: "Jewish studies instructors should study the Talmud for what it conveys about how we can teach our students to be simultaneously critical thinkers and embedded within a particular tradition. […] The Bavli does not force us to choose between critical thinking and authority. Instead, the two speak to one another."*

[75] Greenspahn 2007, 8; Simon 1999, Holtz 2011, 376–77

[76] Greenspahn 2007, 10

[77] Also these assumptions will be discussed in detail in Chapter 3.3

[78] Sommer 2004, 121

In the middle ages, the prevalence of Rabbinic writings over the Hebrew Bible grew to become more and more condescending towards the Written Torah, as some statements of notable Rabbis show: In the 16th centrury, Rabbi Aaron Land defined the Bible as worthless compared to the Talmud while in the 15th, Spanish Rabbis stated how those who only have knowledge about the scripture wouldn't be worthy of a great reward[79] (in an eschatological sense). In the same line of reasoning, Fraade[80] presents a Midrashic commentary on Dtn 17:18-19[81], where the mere text speaking of "law", "scroll", "reading", and "learning" is unfolded to point to Mishnah teaching and Talmudic discussions. Only by this approach to the Law, the fear of God can be achieved:

> From the rabbinical perspective, mere reading of the Written Torah alone is insufficient to bring the king to proper practice and fear of God. It is by dynamically engaging words of Torah, both Written and Oral – trough rabbinic-style study – that the king joins the people in submission to God [...].[82]

According to Greenspahn, the competition coming from the Oral Torah is not the only reason of "the Bible's lowered status in Judaism".[83] The rising influence of Christianity and the increasing hostility towards Rabbinic Judaism contributed to a shift towards the Oral Torah. From the days of the Church Fathers onwards, where Christianity had to negotiate its own identity, Jews had to face the confrontation with arguments coming from their own tradition using documents, which actually would testify the Jewish religious legacy:

> The Church had claimed the Bible for itself. It had to do that to justify itself. The Book, which was a Book of this people and a book for this people, now was to be a book against this people and belong to others.[84]

The consequence of it was that Jews abandoned core elements of their religious life when they saw them to have been appropriated by Christians. In addition, this development nurtured the search for something that was genuinely Jewish and would

[79] Greenspahn 2007, 11

[80] Fraade 2012, 38

[81] When he takes the throne of his kingdom, he is to write for himself on a scroll a copy of this law, taken from that of the Levitical priests. It is to be with him, and he is to read it all the days of his life so that he may learn to revere the Lord his God and follow carefully all the words of this law and these decrees (Dtn 17:18-19, NIV)

[82] Fraade 2012, 41

[83] Greenspahn 2007, 14

[84] Greenspahn 2007, 14 cites Leo Beck: This People Israel 1964, 255

prove the special status of the People of Israel. Greenspahn reports an aggadic passage form Pesikta Rabbati 5 where a dialogue between Moses and God is reported, which predicted how the nations would take over the Torah after having it translated and at that moment they would say that they are Israel. But:

> The Holy One, blessed be He, said to the nations, 'How can you say that you are my children? I only recognize those who have my secret as My child.' They said to Him, 'What is Your secret?' He said to them, 'It is the Mishnah.'[85]

The historical argument why Jews were no longer interested in the Bible reaches its peak after the Christian reformation with the rise of Protestant Bible theology and the historical-critical method in Bible studies. The Bible became the most used "mace" to hit Jews and Jewish beliefs. As a comprehensive study of Gerdman on Protestant bible theology indicates, political antisemitism was nurtured by theological interpretations of biblical exegesis, from the Enlightenment onwards to the first half of the 20th century:

> The picture of Jews and Judaism that biblical interpretation conveyed to the German society for the most part rendered Jewry a place of inferiority and dishonour, even though there are good examples—few but devoted—of strong defence of Jews and Judaism. With its consistent depreciation of Jews and Judaism, the Enlightenment research tradition contributed to this general picture, and salvation-historical scholars, too, agreed to many negative descriptions of Jews and Judaism, as well as pure anti-Semitic stereotypes. But the most intense thought of a strong and fundamental opposition between Judaism and Christianity is found in some salvation-historical scholars, of which several moved into varying degrees of racist depreciation of Jews, including accusations of deicide.[86]

In addition, the historical-critical method, also developed in Christian faculties by Protestant theologians, was perceived as an affront to the Jewish identity. Even in academic settings, Reformed and Conservative Jewish scholars rejected this approach to the Bible as they saw it as a danger to the integrity of the text and questioned the scientific value of biblical criticism itself. Modern methodology for bible-studies was neither taught in Jewish theological seminaries nor in the Hebrew University, at least not in the first period after its foundation.[87] All this contributed to a lack of academic

[85] Greenspahn 2007, 15

[86] Gerdmar 2009, 594

[87] Greenspahn 2007, 18

interest to participate in biblical scholarly work what then resulted in spare publication activity and academic expertise of Jewish thinkers for a discipline concerning what we should consider as the founding document of a nation and religious tradition.

But, on the contrary, the explicit and non-intended hostility of Christian biblical scholars not only contributed to the regression previously described but also invoked, as a reactive response, a rediscovery of the biblical foundations in Jewish thought. This contention will be further addressed in the next subchapter.

4.3 Can you compare Jewish biblical theology to Christian biblical theology?

This master thesis is intended to be written in the field of Old Testament studies within the discipline of biblical theology since it tries to combine scholarly work done on the writings of the Old Testament with philological reference from the history of its reception in order to, in conclusion, formulate general theological considerations. Since the idea of this thesis was generated after an in-class presentation of a book of Benjamin Sommer, I took it for granted that his approach – which would fit perfectly to the theological literature I am used to in my Catholic study program – is common for Jewish studies. The more I began to dive into the research and reading for this project, the more I understood how I was led by another inaccurate preconception on how I would find a matching counterpart to theological disciplines I was used to from my theology program. For the case of biblical theology in Jewish academia, I noticed more and more in the writing process of the thesis how Jewish Bible theology could be still considered a minor discipline – even with a noticeable and high-quality publication output – which continues to struggle to define its methodology and aim foundations.[88]

[88] Sommer 2009, 2, Sweeney 2012, 11–41

But why these reservations? Biblical theology, as a distinct discipline, was founded within the academic Protestant theology[89] in the 18th century.[90] Many textbooks refer to Johann Philipp Gabler as the "father" of the methodology and its distinctive role within the canon of theological disciplines. Since Lutheran theology saw the scripture as the fundamental source for Christian dogmatic, a biblical-theological reflection should constitute the basis for a subsequent dogmatic elaboration. Gabler coined two terms: *true [wahre] biblical theology*, and *pure [reine] biblical theology*. While the true biblical theology is in charge of an accurate historical description of biblical statements, pure biblical theology seeks to identify – trough philosophical reflection – the true underlying ideas of the biblical discourse.[91]

For the reason of the terms used (true, pure) alone, we might be suspicious according to which agenda biblical theology would operate. Indeed, even if we naively assumed that biblical theology would be the discipline par excellence contributing interreligious and ecumenical dialog since it was founded on a shared basis, we see how this academic discipline has been, for most of its history, a stumbling block for other denominations. Especially, the term "biblical" itself is programmatic for a *sola scriptura*[92] condition which is contrary to fundamental understandings of Rabbinic Judaism; the same can be said for the canon of the books: The different collection and order between the Hebrew Tanak and Christian Bible editions stand for a theological objective, which wants to highlight the fulfilment of the Old Testament in Jesus.[93]

---

[89] It might not surprise how most of the critics are directed to Protestant theology. This is not a biased representation of the shared responsibility of all Christian denominations in regard to anti-Semitism, but rather stands for the lack of academic input coming from Catholic Bible studies. Until the Second Vatican Council, the use of state of the art methodologies for the field of biblical studies was highly discouraged or forbidden. Only after 1943, with the Encyclical *Divino afflante Spiritu* a first opening towards contemporary (Protestant) methodology was set, while in 1993, a document from the *Pontifical Biblical Commission* considers the implementation of historical-critical methodology as "irremissible". see Stowasser 2016

[90] Following considerations are formulated on the basis of Merk 1980, 427

[91] *original: ...ist die ‚Wahre Biblische Theologie', welche das Geschäft der historisch sauberen Erforschung der biblischen Aussagen betreibt, von der ‚Reinen Biblischen Theologie', welche durch philosophische Reflexion die wahren Grundideen biblischen Redens ausarbeitet, zu unterscheiden.* Merk 1980, 427

[92] Sommer 2009, 2 Levenson 1987, 285 *...the 'personal stance' of a faithful contemporary Jew does not allow for the isolation of the Jewish Bible (Tanakh) from the larger tradition. Such an isolation is possible on historical grounds, but not on personal, existential grounds.*

[93] Sweeney 2012, 21

On Jewish reservations for biblical theology, Levenson published an essay with the very sharp title *Why Jews Are Not interested in Biblical Theology*.[94] In his contribution, he explains why you there is no Jewish equivalent to Protestant cornerstones of biblical theology, like Eichrodt's *Theology of the Old Testament* (1961) or van Rad's *Old Testament Theology* (1962), which looked for a "Mitte"[95] through the entire Old Testament like a prophetic tradition (van Rad) or the covenant between God an men (Eichrodt). In an introduction to Levenson's theses, Sweeney explains how the different "religious architecture" of Christianity and Judaism contributes, first and foremost, to this lack of interest:

> Judaism does not rely on systematic theology or doctrines in quite the way that Christianity does. Instead, Jewish interpreters pay close attention to the details of the biblical text in an effort to discern the various aspects of its meaning and its impact on Jewish life and thought.[96]

But, also in this case, the biggest share of responsibility is attributed to Protestant biblical theology which – until the aftermath of WWII – engaged mainly in two apologetical discourses[97]: First, in most cases, the Old Testament was seen as preparatory exercise for the New Testament and its fulfilment in Jesus Christ. The old tradition absorbed in a new body and it is only relevant under the introductory perspective since all is fulfilled in the redemption of Jesus Christ. Secondly, a further *topos* in Protestant bible theology was the polemic against a law fixation in Judaism. This discourse is connected to an attribution of spiritual depletion in Jewish religion, which went in the wrong direction. To illustrate this, many essays on this topic refer to Eichrodt's *Theology of the Old Testament,* which – even in 1961 – carried on the *Adversus Judaeos* apologetical discourse[98], which started in the patristic area of Christianity:

> Anyone who studies the historical development of the OT finds that throughout there is a powerful and purposive movement which forces itself on his attention. It is true that there are also times when the religion seems to become static, to harden into a rigid system; [...] This

94 Levenson 1987

95 Sommer 2009, 4 paraphrases this technical term as "a central idea in scripture"

96 Sweeney 2012, 5

97 Levenson 1987, 286–90

98 Today, some of the Christian Bible theology is well aware of the issues of the 'Christianizing' of the Old Testament and aims to reconsider the status of the Old Testament and to engage in a more serious dialog with the Jewish Biblical theology. See Barr 1999, 253-255

movement does not come to rest until the manifestation of Christ, in whom the noblest powers of the OT find their fulfilment. Negative evidence in support of this statement is afforded by the torso-like appearance of Judaism in separation from Christianity.[99]

As mentioned in the last sentences of the previous chapter, the Christian hostility not only produced hesitations among many Jews to engage in this field but also challenged others to get involved and counter. As Solomon Schechter addressed in 1903:

> ...this intellectual persecution can only be fought by intellectual weapons and unless we make an effort to recover our Bible and to think out our theology for ourselves, we are irrevocably lost from both worlds.[100]

In fact, neither Levenson's essay itself nor the contributions of Sweeny or Sommer prove that Jews did not engage in biblical theology since all their papers contain an anthology of modern and contemporary publications allocated to this domain. Rather, the main difference consists in the academic approach: While Protestant theology was concerned to find *a* central topic to formulate a theology for the entire Old Testament (with the perspective towards the New Testament), Jewish scholarship mostly set a research question and examined how the topic (messianism, monotheism, relationship between Good and men, etc.) is unfolded within the Hebrew Bible and postbiblical writings. This approach is meant to meet the diversity of voices of the vast biblical tradition and bring them together in a dialog.[101]

Some of these contributions[102] are seen as a Jewish counterdraft to Protestant inimicality, like Kaufmann's historical-critical theology of the Hebrew Bible, who brought the Temple and the priesthood back to the centre of the continuing religious history of Israel. Other contributions deal with the experience of the Shoah and the rising question of theodicy. Hence, Emil Frackenheim's *God's Presence in History* is introduced with biblical integration arguing for the Shoah as an analogous catastrophe

---

[99] Eichrodt 1961, 26. Benjamin Sommer comments on it: *When Eichrodt describes rabbinic legalism as dead and stultifying, he does not merely offend Jews. More troublingly, he jettisons any pretensions of scholarship, since description of rabbinic religiosity is based neither on textual analyses of rabbinic literature nor sociological investigations of living rabbinic communities. Rather, his description is found in Pauline and late Christian literature.* Sommer 2009, 8

[100] Levenson 1987, 290 cites Higher Criticism – Higher Anti-Semitism," in: Salomon Schechter, Seminary Address and Other Papers, Cincinnati: Ark Publishing 1915.

[101] Sweeney 2016, 315; Sommer 2009, 50–51

[102] References and introductions have been taken from Sweeney 2012, 12–20

to the destruction of both, the First and Second Temple, and the Babylonian Exile and the resulting human obligation to work as partners of God to complete the creation and sanctification of the world. Modern and contemporary Jewish scholarly, which Sweeny counts along Jewish Bible theology, aims to reconnect modern Jews with the Jewish tradition. Among these the most prominent authors are Martin Buber, Franz Rosenzweig, and Joshua Heschel with dynamic models for a contemporary understanding of how Jewish scripture can still be central for a modern Jew. In fact, and this will be analysed in detail in the next chapter, not only historical and biographical events like the ongoing anti-Semitism and its culmination in the Shoah harmed Jewish religious live, but also a growing secularization and the rise of empirical epistemology made it harder for Jews to believe in transcendental commands, like the divine nature of the Torah. In this respect, Jewish biblical theology shares a task with contemporary Christian biblical theology. But what could biblical theology in the 21th century look like? Sommer postulates following aims and methodological perspectives:

> An approach that allows us to read it [the Bible] as scripture while integrating what we know about it as an artefact. [...] Modern religious people who reject willful *naivitè* clearly require an approach to scripture that is once academically critical and religiously engaged, and that approach might well be called biblical theology.[103]

[103] Sommer 2009, 20

5 Participatory Revelation in Judaism

In this extended chapter, the concept of participatory revelation within the work of Benjamin Sommer is presented. Exegetical considerations on the Sinai pericope (Ex 19-24) are meant to address how the biblical text itself supports the thesis of a human involvement in the shaping of the authoritative text with its commandments and laws. An introduction to the thoughts of three of the most relevant Jewish philosophers of modern times – Rosenzweig, Buber, and Heschel – provides the background knowledge to reconstruct ideas of contemporary biblical theology. Sommer's understanding of a participatory revelation in Judaism is presented through the lens of three theses.

Even if Rabbinic Judaism infrequently developed a systematic chart of dogmatic principles – compared to Christian denominations –, one list containing 13 principles of faith had success and is being used by believers still today[104]: In the commentary on the Mishnah (tractate Sanhedrin), Rabbi Moses Maimonides (1135-1204 CE) summarized what is essential for the Jewish Faith into 13 positions. The eighth principle states that the Torah is from heaven, it was given to Moses by God, it came as a "speech". Even if scholars warn to read in Maimonides a concept of a literal dictation of the words of the Torah – since it contradicts crucial philosophical assumptions of Maimonides[105] – this formulation from the most brilliant Jewish thinker of all times has been received as the basis for a "stenographic" understanding. The *stenographic theory of revelation* is a term used to indicate positions which see Moses (and other Prophets) as secretaries, which would compose the biblical text by accurately transcribing what they received as revelations by God. Mostly, adherents of a stenographic theory are opposed to any considerations that would imply that the scripture contains a human component. Such approaches are not outdated since, even in modern times, there still can be found supporters for these theories: In 1966, the editors of the *Commentary Magazine* submitted five questions to 55 leading Rabbis from Orthodox, Conservative, and Reformed traditions. The first question addressed was:

> In what sense do you believe the Torah to be divine revelation? Are all 613 commandments equally binding on the believing Jew? If not, how is he to decide which to observe?[106]

Various Rabbis expressed views, which try to actualize the understanding of divine origin to fit it to a modern understanding, which might struggle with the

[104] see https://www.chabad.org/library/article_cdo/aid/332555/jewish/Maimonides-13-Principles-of-Faith.htm [15.04.2018]

[105] Fleischacker 2014

[106] Commentary Magazine 1966

assumption of a complete heavenly origin. Others, like the Orthodox Rabbi Norman Lamm (*1927), responded in defence of a verbal revelation of the Torah:

> Hence, I accept unapologetically the idea of the verbal revelation of the Torah. I do not take seriously the caricature of this idea which reduces Moses to a secretary taking dictation. [...] Exactly how this communication took place no one can say; it is no less mysterious than the nature of the One who spoke. The divine-human encounter is not a meeting of equals, and the *kerygma* that ensues from this event must therefore be articulated in human terms without reflecting on the mode and form of the divine *logos.* How God spoke is a mystery; how Moses received this message is irrelevant. [...] To deny that God can make His will clearly known is to impose upon Him a limitation of dumbness that would insult the least of His human creatures.

Literary criticism of the Bible is a problem, but not a crucial one. Judaism has successfully met greater challenges in the past.[107]

About the same time, Rabbi Jacob Louis, who became one of the most influential Conservative Rabbis in Britain, challenged a naive understanding of the 8th principle according to Maimonides and wrote on biblical revelation:

> Revelation . . . is not the communication of *words* to man, not a divine dictation to a passive human recipient, but a meeting of God and man in history, a meeting producing results of eternal significance. . . . That the record is humanly mediated, that it is colored by its human background and the minds of its human authors, that it contains error as well as truth, does not affect its claim, or the claim made for it in Jewish tradition, to contain the word of God. We must stress the word "contain" for the new view of revelation—of "Torah from heaven"—is that it is *contained* in the Bible, not that the Bible itself is revelation. The words are human, they have a history, there are contradictions and discrepancies in them . . . but, for all that, in this collection of books, as in no other, the account is there for all to read how man found God and how God helped man to find him.[108]

The voices of 1966 are very similar to the publications of the last decades where some theologians continued to push for a stenographic model (used as a synonym for dictation or verbal inspiration) while others tried to continuously develop formulations which, following a model of participated revelation, aim to deliver a theological framework more suited to the demands of contemporary believers.

[107] Commentary Magazine 1966

[108] Jacobs 1964 cited by Potok 1965

Indeed, scholars like Benjamin Sommer try to reconcile "two souls": the soul of a believer seeking to find a religious message in the sacred text and the academic soul which – embracing historical and critical methodology – sees the Bible as an ancient cultural artefact. For this, *Revelation and Authority – Sinai in Jewish Scripture and Tradition*[109] – the book at the centre of this master thesis – can be categorized as belonging to the field of dialogical Bible theology aiming to integrate biblical scholar work with philosophical and theological traditions.[110] But, what is the target? The first aim might be confined to a mere academic endeavour, „which is whether one can, with intellectual integrity and consistency, believe at once in revelation at Sinai and in biblical criticism“[111]. A second scope has wider practical implications for the religious life; modern Bible readers often struggle with passages they cannot reconcile with their belief in a merciful God or with basic ethical principles, like commands to slaughter all Amalekites including their children (Dtn 25:17-19), incitations for a genocide towards the Canaanites (Dtn 7:1) or recurring considerations understood in a misogynist or homophobic way. According to Sommer, the main object in undertaking a project to develop a model for a more appropriate understanding of divine origin is connected with practical issues of contemporary believers:

> Moral issues rather than historical-philological ones pose the most disturbing challenge to the Bible's status of scripture. I am not alone in this respect. To many a modern Jew, the Tenakh is a hallowed book but also an embarrassing one. However much we revere it, we are aware of its human side.[112]

In his opening remarks, Sommer reminds the reader that a concept of participatory revelation is neither his or *his* invention nor it is a purely modern endeavour. Referring to recent publications of the Israeli scholar Eran Viezel[113], the view on the Pentateuch as "a mixture of divine and human elements that include not only God's own words but also, and more frequently, Moses's own words"[114] was widely accepted among Jewish thinkers of the middle ages, in particular by the prominent Jewish philosophers

[109] Sommer 2015

[110] Brill 2015, Sommer 2009

[111] Sommer 2017

[112] Sommer 2015, 28

[113]Dr. Eran Viezel teaches at the Ben Gurion University of the Negev in Be'er Sheva where I had an opportunity to talk to him about my master project. Unfortunately, the works Sommer is referring to are only published in Hebrew and, therefore could not be included in this work.

[114] Sommer 2015, 2–3

ibn Ezra (1092-1167) and Rashbam (1085-1158). With modesty, Sommer defines his work on revelation as "nothing more than a long footnote to the work of liberal theologians like Heschel, Rosenzweig, and Louis Jacobs, and in other respects a footnote to Solomon Schechter and Zachariah Frankel"[115], but at the same time, in his work, he combines biblical studies, Jewish philosophy, and modern theology which often have been kept separated.

The following two chapters will briefly introduce some of the background knowledge and key arguments derived from biblical scholarship (chapter 3.1) and modern Jewish philosophers (chapter 3.2), which are necessary to understand the synthesis created in Sommer's work. Sommer's view of *Participatory Revelation* will be introduced in chapter 3.3 through three concepts, which – from a Christian perspective – seem to be crucial for the Jewish discourse and at the same time informative for Christian theology.

5.1 Exegetical Considerations: The Ambiguity of Sinai

A key aspect of all considerations on a concept of revelation consists in a systematic analysis of the biblical text. All speculations and argumentative attempts start with what is often referred to as "The Sinai Theophany" situated in Exodus 19-24. Beginning with the narration in Ex 18, Israel dwells in the desert and Moses camped near the Mountain of God (הר האלהים Ex 18,5). In Chapter 19, the desert and the mount are named Sinai while in Ex 33,6 the mountain where the theophany and lawgiving took place is called Horeb.[116] Before we delve into what Sommer defines as "ambiguity of Sinai"[117], we should begin with some general considerations on biblical criticism on the Sinai pericope. Indeed, these five chapters are a clear composition and "a mine of information" for source criticism.[118] In the narrative and legal elements of the text, we can identify several doublets, contradictions, redactions, and inconsistent

[115] Brill 2015

[116] Oswald 2014, 169 However, חורב must not be considered as a proper term but might only indicate the wasteland where the mountain was located.

[117] Sommer 2015, 35

[118] Collins 2004, 124. See, for example, from a feminist perspective Plaskow 2008, 108: *There is no revelation without interpretation; the foundational experience of revelation also involves a crucial act of interpretation. Second, we learn that the process of interpretation is ongoing. What Moses does, the Rabbis in this case seek to undo. While they reiterate and reinforce the exclusion of women in many contexts, they mitigate it in others.*

narrations. Even if the redactors did not wholly harmonize the elements, the text is well structured with narrative elements introducing and legitimizing legal elements, people, and social functions.[119]

Sprinkle[120] identifies a chiastic structure with alternating narrative and legalistic components following the purpose to assign a primacy to the Decalogue and, at the same time, to outline the centrality of the covenant rather than of singular laws:

A. Narrative: The covenant offered (Exod 19:3–25)
  B. Laws (general): The Decalogue (Exod 20:1–17)
    C. Narrative: The people's fear (Exod 20:18–21)
  B* Laws (specific): The book of the covenant (Exod 20:22–23:33)
A* Narrative: The covenant accepted (Exod 24:1–11)

Oswald[121], on the other hand, outlines a structure with the focus on the purpose of the narrative to set the basis of Israel's constitution with its law and judiciary system.

Two-level directive structure: judges and Mosaic office (18:13–26 as part of 18:1–27)
  Preparation of the people; preliminary treaty; theophany before the people (19:1–25)
    Two-level law system: basic commitments ("Decalogue," 20:1–17)
      Separation of the two levels (20:18–21)
    Two-level law system: detailed law book ("Covenant Code," 20:22–23:33)
  Resolution of the people; definite treaty; consecration of the people (24:3–8)
Two-level directive structure: gerousia; deputies to Moses; more laws announced (24:1–2, 9–18)

The question of legitimization is also central in source criticism where, according to the documentary hypothesis, four traditions can be found in the Five Books of the Torah: the Elohist, Jahwist, Priestly, and Deuteronomistic. From the first verse onwards, the Sinai pericope confronts the reader with doublets and inconsistent narration so that first hypotheses can be generated regarding which traditions a certain passage can be allocated to. The "movements" of Moses, up and down the mountain, are in fact curious – or even hilarious – if we read them as the narrative sequence presents it:

[119] For in-depth analyses on how the Sinai pericope was applied for the shaping of social orders, especially in gender issues, see Najman 2003 and Plaskow 1990

[120] Sprinkle 2004, 242

[121] Oswald 2014, 171–73

These texts present a bewildering aggregate of verses de-scribing Moses's ascents and descents on the mountain. Moses seems not to be located at the right place when the Decalogue is given: God tells him to descend the mountain and then re-ascend with Aaron (Exodus 19.24), whereupon he descends (19.25); but before he reascends, the revelation of the law takes place (20.1). Similarly, we may ask, where is God located before and during the revelation? According to Exodus 19.3, God is on the mountain several days before this event, but according to 19.11, God descends to the mountain immediately prior to the theophany (in agreement with 19.18); yet in 19.20 Yhwh comes down to the summit again.[122]

Furthermore, we find additional inconsistencies if we focus on who has been ordered by God to ascend to the Mountain versus those for who it is prohibited to do so. According to Ex 19,24, Moses would have had to take his brother Aaron (who became first high-priest) with him while the priests and the people should not attempt to climb the mountain. In Ex 24,1[123], Aaron, Nadab and Abihu, and seventy of the elders of Israel should ascent the mountain with Moses. On the contrary, Ex 24,13, after in v12 God (re)ordered Moses to climb the Mountain even though he and the 73 others already were there, the Prophet was accompanied by his assistant Joshua while Aaron stood with the 70 elder on the ground. Considering that Aaron and his sons Nadab and Abihu are central in the corpus of Priestly laws (Ex 25-40, Lev, and Num[124]; see Ex 28 and 29) while Joshua is deeply connected with the Deuteronomistic History, we can hypothesize how different sources tried to legitimize concurring moral and political authorities.[125]

To sum up, we have to consider that first results derived from source criticism pleading for a participatory concept of revelation: the plurality of the narration and the attempts to legitimize the own tradition by connecting it to the event of Sinai show how human, cultural adaptation of a transcendental event is most prominent – even in the pericope, which stands for the moment of divine revelation!

Moving now from some general remarks derived from biblical criticism towards a content-based, synchronic observation, we continue to discuss the ambiguity of the

[122] Sommer 2015, 32

[123] According to Sommer 2015, 41, there are different opinions on Ex 24 whether it narrates the same events or discusses events preceding or following the theophany of Ex 19.

[124] Collins 2004, 139

[125] Dozeman 1989, 183 indicates how the emphasis on Aaron is a late contribution by the priestly theologians. For Joshua, however, I was not able to find any studies linking him to his political importance or to a Deuteronomist redaction.

revelation on Sinai. A naïve understanding of revelation and law-giving, as it is the base for a *stenographic revelation*, would imply that all the words contained in the Torah are of divine origin and those who assisted the revelation, so mainly Moses and possibly a few others, accurately wrote down what was revealed to them, thus creating the books of the Torah. As a result, a distinct moment could be identified where God clearly spoke to a human person – possibly for a period long enough to communicate the vast extension of the Torah text – in order to facilitate the writing process.

Even if these last speculations are intentionally exaggerated, they aim to emphasize how many assumptions must be fulfilled in order to make a "stenographic" understanding plausible. On the other hand, especially in the light of evidence derived from biblical criticism, a comprehensive understanding of the instances where a human reception and interpretation process of a transcendental experience occurred is not only more logical in fostering a general comprehension, but also more suited for what the Sinai pericopes in Exodus and Deuteronomy report.

To prove this assumption, Sommer identifies five ambiguities[126] for the events reported in Ex 19-20, which will be introduced and briefly discussed in the following chapter.

5.1.1 The emphasis on visual elements

First, like a premise, Sommer points out how strongly these chapters emphasize on visual events. Ex 19,16 reports thunder and lightning, a thick cloud, and a very loud trumpet blast. Verse 18 reports smoke, "because the Lord descended on it in fire" and an earthquake. Other biblical books took up these events with our without explicit mentioning of the connection to the revelation on Sinai: Judges 5,4-5 *When you, Lord, went out from Seir, when you marched from the land of Edom, the earth shook, the heavens poured, the clouds poured down water. The mountains quaked before the Lord, the One of Sinai, before the Lord, the God of Israel* and Ps 68,7-8 *When you, God, went out before your people, when you marched through the wilderness, the earth shook, the heavens poured down rain, before God, the One of Sinai, before God, the God of Israel* mention Sinai and the natural events, while other passages (like Ps 50,

[126] Sommer 2015, 30–41

1-7; Hab 3,3-6; Ps 114) refrain on explicitly referring to the events on Sinai; however, they show how the manifestation of God is connected with frightening natural powers.

For this the first ambiguity deals with the meaning of the word קוֹל, which in Ex 19,16 and 20,18 is translated as *thunder*, while in verse 5 this root is part of the expression תשמעו בקלי, which is translated to *if you obey me.* Sommer aims to highlight how קוֹל, which in other contexts means voice, is associated here with a powerful sound of a natural event. The command to obey, at least how the biblical narrative plays with the semantical meaning of this word, is not given by the sound of a human voice but trough a powerful natural event. This ambiguity becomes even more clear in Ex 19,19, where the NIV translates *[...] Moses spoke and the voice of God answered him*[127] with a footnote: or *"and God answered him with thunder".*

5.1.2 Direct or mediated communication

In consequence to the first consideration, the question arises: What did the nation hear? In order to try and find and answer, one must consider first the reaction of the people reported in Ex 20,18 consecutive to the Decalogue:

> 18When the people saw the thunder and lightning and heard the trumpet and saw the mountain in smoke, they trembled with fear. They stayed at a distance 19and said to Moses, "Speak to us yourself and we will listen. But do not have God speak to us or we will die."

Therefore, a general understanding implies that the nation heard the Decalogue entirely "and when the Decalogue ended, the nation asked to be spared of more direct revelations"[128], so that all the following laws in Ex 20.23-23.33 are given by Mosaic mediation. In contrast, Sommer presents an alternative reading according to which, conforming to the particular syntactical construction of Ex 20,18[129], it is plausible that the nation heard the Decalogue partially or even all of it mediated by Moses. This supposition has to be kept in mind when discussing for which section of the biblical texts a human participation might be assumed.

---

[127] משה ידבר והאלהים יעננו בקול:

[128] Sommer 2015, 37

[129] *The absence in 20.18 of the typical past tense of biblical narratives (the waw-consecutive) is unusual, and the syntax here (waw + noun + participle) normally indicates that the event reported was simultaneous with a previously narrated occurance. The syntax suggests that the conversation between Moses and the people took place during the giving of the Decalogue; the narrator avoids interruption the text of the commandments, however, and thus the narrative does not begin again until Exodus 20.18* Sommer 2015, 37

5.1.3 Additions and text variants

The third ambiguity Sommer identifies for the Sinai pericope is also related to the Decalogue and how it is introduced. Ex 20,1 וַיְדַבֵּר אֱלֹהִים אֵת כָּל־הַדְּבָרִים הָאֵלֶּה לֵאמֹר׃ uses a construction with a waw-consecutive for דבר (spoke) and אמר (said), which is common for biblical text, but in this case a particle indicating to whom God is speaking is missing. In Sommer's words: "Only in this verse introducing the Decalogue in Exodus is there any doubt about the recipient of divine speech. This fact is jarring to an audience whose ears are familiar with hundreds of cases of the normal form".[130] For this, ancient translations added a prepositional object, as can be read in the variant apparatus for Ex 20,1[131]:

1 Καὶ ἐλάλησεν Κύριος πάντας τοὺς λόγους τούτους λέγων

XX 1 ⟨και ελαλησεν κυριος] κ̅ς̅ δε ο θ̅ς̅ ελαλησε 30⟩ | om και m Spec | κυριος] ο θ̅ς̅ F^{b}: + ο θ̅ς̅ ackn: + προς μωυσην Ay 𝔈^{c}: + *ad populum* 𝔏 | ⟨om παντας 30⟩ | ⟨τουτους] + προς μωυσην 83⟩

The Vetus Latina adds *to the people* while Codex Alexandrinus reads *to Moses* along with other minor manuscripts. However, the Hebrew text does not explicitly indicate the recipients of the Decalogue; therefore, the question of direct vs. mediated revelation, also for the Decalogue, still needs to be discussed.

5.1.4 Direct speech or narration

In support of this, another ambiguity is reported. If we read chapters 19 and 20 the narration seems not to be coherent due to the punctuation, which results in either Moses not standing on the mountain but hearing the Revelation of the Decalogue, or, with a different punctuation, the direct speech would be changed to an indirect one. Modern translations, here the NIV, use following punctuation for Ex 19.25-20.2:

> 25So Moses went down to the people and told them. 1And God spoke all these words: 2"I am the Lord your God, who brought you out of Egypt, out of [...]

[130] Sommer 2015, 38

[131] The Old Testament in Greek 1906/2010, 219

At the same time, the punctuation could be changed to "and told them: "And God spoke all these words 'I am the Lord....' " letting Moses report the Decalogue and not the narrator. For both readings, Sommer finds arguments in support and against. In a footnote he sums up and speaks of "at the least a very unusual use of the verb that avoids the clarity"[132].

5.1.5 Seeing the thunder

The last ambiguity reported here deals with a paradoxical formulation in Ex 20.18, which was and is heavily discussed in exegesis and has been subject to analysis earlier in this paper but for another aspect:

> When the people saw the thunder and lightning and heard the trumpet and saw the mountain in smoke, they trembled with fear. They stayed at a distance.[18]

How can thunder, a sound, be seen? Through the centuries, interpreters from different traditions tried to explain this odd use of ראים either through a naturalistic understanding, where the presence of God's voice/thunder shaped the nature[133], or as referring to a perception, which cannot be accurately described in the human language. Contemporary interpretations, as Barton's study shows, focus on this perplexing metaphor and read the text as an invitation for a deeper "process of understanding the meaning of each commandment, rather than to the sensory perception of the divine voice."[134]

To sum up, this subchapter aimed to report biblical work done on the Sinai pericope, which shows how even in the most central text on revelation the biblical text is quite ambiguous. By doing this, we can point out how theological and philosophical speculations on a contemporary understanding of revelation are supported by the features of the biblical text. To some extent it seems that the text invites readers and scholars to engage in a more sophisticated understanding of what an intuitive, superficial reading would propose. From the perspective of biblical studies, a hypothesis for a participated process of revelation can be supported through the text of the Exodus.

---

[132] Sommer 2015, 269

[133] Barton 2011, 14 cites here Saadia Gaon, a Babylonian exegist form the 9th century.

[134] Barton 2011, 15

5.2 Philosophical Foundations

As second building brick for introducing a theology of participated revelation, some philosophical positions as predecessors of contemporary thought on participatory need to be discussed first. Indeed, Sommer's work shows how many philosophers and scholars, even in the middle ages, contributed to the notion of a participated revelation. However, three modern Jewish thinkers have to be highlighted separately: Franz Rosenzweig, Martin Buber, and Abraham Joshua Heschel. In order to introducing their thoughts and their concepts of revelation adequately, an entire thesis would have to be written. For this subchapter, a brief outline using secondary sources and some quotations of primary works of these famous Jewish thinkers should set the basis to understand contemporary concepts like the work of Benjamin Sommer.

In the introduction of *The State of Jewish Belief*, Himmelfarb points out the importance of Rosenzweig and Buber in shaping the Jewish thought in the 20th century and comparing Buber to Maimonides:

> Buber was the first Jewish religious thinker since Maimonides eight centuries ago who was able to influence Christian theology, and his thought might therefore have been expected to benefit among Jews not only from its own merit but also from its prestige among Christians. Yet as between Buber and Rosenzweig, close associates in the 1920's, it is Rosenzweig, fated to die young, and ignored by Christians, who dominates non-Orthodox Jewish theology; and it is Buber, who died full of years, and honored in Christian theology, whose influence on Jews is relatively slight.[135]

In fact, Buber is often quoted in Sommer's work, but also criticized since latter argues that the former offers a frameset which is less appropriate for supporting his theses[136], but has to be mentioned as his influence, implicit or explicit, cannot be ignored. In this subchapter, I would like to introduce Rosenzweig's and Buber's contemplations and report in detail on Heschel's notions on revelation.

---

[135] Editors of Commentary Magazine 1966

[136] In footnotes, Sommer 2015, 264 indicates how Buber's mere focus on the presence of God rather than on content and deriving obligation makes him less relevant in discussing issues of authority resulting from revelation.

5.2.1 Franz Rosenzweig and The Star of Redemption

Franz Rosenzweig, 1886-1929, was a German philosopher born to liberal-Jewish parents. To his biography two facts should be mentioned: As many other German Jews of that time, he and his family where fully assimilated to German society and he, as his correspondence indicates[137], was pondering converting to Christianity but opted then consciously to remain Jew (*Ich bleibe also Jude)* and rediscovered Judaism for himself through an existentialist approach. His best-known work is *The Star of Redemption*, published in German as *Der Stern der Erlösung* in 1921, which Pollock introduces as "arguably the greatest work of modern Jewish philosophy"[138]. The core of his contemplations in *The Start* is that God is "transcendent to and independent of the human being in the world, at once enters into relation with the human being in the world"[139] and thus breaking with the at that time popular rationalistic approach of reducing God to a projection of humans for a Jewish aspiration of unity. Creation, revelation, and redemption are understood as relations between God and humans, which change the human existence and their orientation. The existentialist, neo-Hegelian approach, as Pollock[140] introduces Rosenzweig's work, makes it hard to formulate concise concepts for his thoughts. As Harhowitz refers to it regarding his notion on dialog and revelation: "One can find a lack of consistency, sometimes tending more towards a mystical type of speechless encounter and at other times emphasizing speech"[141]. However, we should consider some notions of Rosenzweig in how he draws the attention to the existential revelation moment, rather to a literal wording of the law in the Torah, but at the same time still understands the law as fundamental for Jewish life.

In *Star of Redemption* we see how, in Rosenzweig's mind, revelation is mere self-disclosure, something that could be called an epiphany:

---

[137] Pollock 2014

[138] Pollock 2015

[139] Pollock 2015

[140] Pollock 2015

[141] Harhowitz 1989, 358

> Das Offenbarwerden, das wir hier suchen, muß ein solches sein, das ganz wesentlich Offenbarung ist und nichts weiter; das heißt aber: es darf nichts sein als das Sichauftun eines Verschlossenen.[142]

This view is reinforced by a fragment commenting on a poem, as reported in an edition created by his student Glatzer:

> All that God ever reveals in revelation is—revelation. Or, to express it differently, he reveals nothing but himself to man. The relation of this accusative and dative to each other is the one and only content of revelation. Whatever does not follow directly from this covenant between God and man, whatever cannot prove its direct bearing on this covenant, cannot be a part of it.[143]

It might not surprise that Rosenzweig develops a philosophical, theological system around the concept of love and, therefore, focuses on a personal, individual sphere. In the words of Harhowitz: "The command of God is always to a particular human being; it can never be a universal rule".[144] So, if law is seen as fundamental in Jewish life[145], how can his focus on the individual, existential level be connected to tradition? Can there be a distinction between divine and human elements? Also in secondary literature, attempts to answer these basic doubts are unsystematical and in part confusing. But for the reception of Rosenzweig's thoughts, two main assumption can be identified: Rosenzweig identifies the authority of Law but, in the light of his "New Thinking", he bypasses it[146] with the focus on the individual responsibility deriving from the personal relationship with God:

> Rosenzweig's understanding of the law differs from both the Reform and the Orthodox [meaning adherents to Reformed and Orthodox Judaism]. Whereas the Reform decide publicly which laws are important and which can be discarded, Rosenzweig thinks that this decision should be private and individual. He himself accepted only parts of halakhah, but he did not wish to publicize the details.[147]

To sum up, in Rosenzweig's writing we find an existential approach based on a complex philosophical system that understands revelation as an indescribable encounter between God and men. In consequence, whatever has been revealed and

---

[142] Rosenzweig 1921, 179

[143] Rosenzweig and Glatzer 1961, 285

[144] Harhowitz 1989, 359

[145] For an ambivalent but, in comparison to Buber, major emphasis on the importance of law as it "reorientates the individual" see Batnitzsky 2006, 152

[146] Batnitzsky 2006, 163

[147] Harhowitz 1989, 363

later written is always a midrash, a reflection and interpretation of a self-disclosure of God.[148]

5.2.2 Martin Buber and the Dialogical Philosophy

The name Martin Buber (1878-1965) is often recalled in the same breath with Rosenzweig since they shared an intellectual collaboration and educational practice. It was Rosenzweig who recruited Buber for the *Freies Jüdisches Lehrhaus* in Frankfurt as a lecturer in Jewish religious studies and ethics.[149] Born in Vienna 1878, Buber spent only his early childhood in the capital of the Austro-Hungarian Empire and moved at the age of four, after the separation of his parents, to Lemberg in Galicia (taday Lviv in the Ukraine) where he got in contact with the Zionist movement, and the literature as well spirituality of Hassidism.

His best-known work is undoubtedly *I and Thou* (Ich und Du), which was published in 1923. It is one of the most influential works within the Philosophy of Dialogue with the central thesis of dialogical relationships established between the three expressive signifiers[150] "I", "You", and "It". These primary words are never singular, isolated words, but always combined: I-Thou, I-It.[151] While I-It stands for a subject-object relation, an utilitarian interest, and follows logical criteria of verification and falsification, I-Thou is characterized by a "dialogical immediacy".[152] Buber thinks dialogical relations not only to occur between humans but also between other beings, animals and nature, and also with the Divine Thou. Katz characterises the I-Thou relation as subjective, as a meeting in the awareness of the other as a subject, respecting his autonomy; it is based on mutuality so that "the symmetry of relation is a basic premise of the whole dialogical life."[153]

From this perspective, Buber describes also the relationship between men and God, which has to be a genuine encounter as I and Thou, since the reduction of God to an It, with the attempt to analyse and describe his nature contradict his very

[148] Sommer 2015, 29; Harhowitz 1989, 363

[149] Zank and Braiterman 2014

[150] Zank and Braiterman 2014

[151] Buber 1973, 7

[152] Katz 1978, 58,, some of the wording used is also derived from this article.

[153] Katz 1978, 59–60

essence.[154] So how can revelation be thought of in this context? According to Katz[155], "dialogue is really another name for 'revelation'" so that this term does not uniquely apply to the event on Sinai but is persisting and, as "it is assimilated to this inter-subjective dialogic model 'revelation' is denied all 'content and therefore it cannot be claimed that God is a legislator or revealer of anything reassembling the doctrines of positive religion." According to Buber's thesis, revelation focuses on presence instead of a content:

> Man receives, and he receives not a specific "content" but a Presence, a Presence as power. This Presence and this power include three things, undivided, yet in such a way that we may consider them separately. First, there is the whole fulness of real mutual action, of the being raised and bound up in relation : [...] Secondly, there is the inexpressible confirmation of meaning. Meaning is assured. Nothing can any longer be meaningless. [...] Thirdly, this meaning is not that of " another life ", but that of this life of ours, not one of a world " yonder " but that of this world of ours, and it desires its confirmation in this life and in relation with this world.[156]

The same motive can be found in his writings on biblical topics. Buber not only contributed with a translation of the Hebrew Bible to German, in collaboration with Rosenzweig, but also reflected some biblical issues in brief essays, which have been published in several editions. In "On the Bible", an edition compiled by Nahun N. Glatzer, we discover some notions which reflect Buber's thought:

For Buber, the "theme of the Bible is the encounter between a group of people and the Lord of the world in the course of history"[157] for which it would be wrong to reduce it to a religious purpose:

> If we accept the Old Testament as merely religious writing, as a subdivision of the detached spirit, it will fail us, we must needs fail it. If we seize upon it as the expression of the reality that comprises all of life, we really grasp it, and it grasps hold of us.[158]

In the same line of thought he continues discussing what is revelation, refuting a punctual fixation to a single event: "The Revelation at Sinai is not the midpoint itself,

[154] Buber 1973, 113

[155] Katz 1978, 60

[156] Buber 1973, 1101 Translation of Smith (1937, 110), retrieved from: *https://archive.org/details/IAndThou_572* (8.3.2018)

[157] Buber 1968, 1

[158] Buber 1968, 4

but the perceiving of it, and such perception is possible at any time"[159] with the consequence that other biblical books not connected with the event at Sinai, as the Psalms, are elevated to an equal status of the Torah. But, on the level of commandment and laws, how does Buber's view affect their authority? In line with his philosophy of dialog, Buber reports on a thesis of Goethe proposing his assumption that "the history and doctrine of the people of Israel had a particularistic and not a universal character"[160] catching up with this thesis in his focus on the semantics of the formulation of the Decalogue:

> The Ten Commandments are not part of an impersonal codex governing an association of men. They were uttered by an *I* and addressed to a *Thou.* They begin with the I and every one of them addresses the Thou in person.[161]

In brief, even if Buber's dialogical approach offers a philosophical basis for a participated concept of revelation, most of the questions about the extend and the possibilities of how this interaction between God and human took place will not be answered. Indeed, also because of Buber's radical existential approach, which refuses to rationalize a dialogical interaction, this "project" of participated revelation, as Sommer calls it[162], would not be discussed including a historical-critical approach to the biblical text but only be labelled as "presence".

5.2.3 Abraham J. Heschel – Prophecy as a model

In contrast, *Abraham Jeshua Heschel* presents a model, which focuses more on the process between the revelation and the words becoming the biblical text. Born in Warsaw in 1907, Heschel is considered to be a descendant of important Hasidic dynasties and was familiar with these streams of mystical revival movements.[163] After a traditional Jewish education in local yeshivas, he continued his studies at the University of Berlin where – in 1932 – he received his doctorate with a thesis on Biblical Prophecy. Sweeny[164] mentions this thesis as revolutionary for that period where biblical studies were dominated by critical-historical methods, while Heschel's

---

[159] Buber 1968, 3

[160] Buber 1968, 94

[161] Buber 1968, 118

[162] Sommer 2015, 264

[163] Seltzer 1980

[164] Sweeney 2012, 13

work was instead characterized by a reflection on the status of the prophets through receiving God's revelation and how this changed their existence. In fact, his theological contributions are marked by the focus on the subjective human situation and the encounter with something supernatural and transcendent and by the rejection of refuting psychological or other rationalistic reductionism on religion.[165]

Central to Herschel's work is the topic of the encounter between God and men, which is essential to understand the nature of the revelation and the Torah. In his studies *Man is Not Alone*[166] and *God in Search of Man*[167] he outlines his understanding on how religion and belief can be understood in terms of encounter and how they are "defined as the answer to man's ultimate questions"[168]. Accordingly, the understanding of the biblical text changes and with it the approach to reading and discussing them:

> We must not try to read chapters in the Bible dealing with the event at Sinai as if they were texts in systematic theology. Its intention is to celebrate the mystery, to introduce us to it rather than to penetrate or to explain it. As report about revelation the Bible itself is *a midrash*.[169]

What is *revelation* for Heschel? In *God in Search of Man,* he stresses how revelation is and remains a mystery, "something which words cannot spell"[170] and "empirical categories would have produced a caricature"[171]. He points out, how also inner-biblical exegesis, like the Elija narrative in 1 Kings 19, prefers to use a *via negationis* and to express how the event of the revelation cannot be fixed to an element or empirical category:

> "Go out and stand on the mountain in the presence of the LORD, for the LORD is about to pass by."
> Then a great and powerful wind tore the mountains apart and shattered the rocks before the LORD, but the LORD was not in the wind. After the wind there was an earthquake, but the LORD was not in the earthquake.
> 12 After the earthquake came a fire, but the LORD was not in the fire. And after the fire came a gentle whisper. 13 When Elijah heard it, he pulled his cloak over his face and went out and stood at the mouth of the cave. (1 Kings 19:11-12, NIV)

165 Rothschild and Meir 2007; Heschel 1956, 184

166 Heschel 1951

167 Heschel 1956

168 Rothschild and Meir 2007

169 Heschel 1956, 185

170 Heschel 1956, 184

171 Heschel 1956, 185

To outline how revelation could be apprehended he introduces a clear distinction between a mystic act and God's revelation to the prophets. While a mystic act is induced and an active search for an esoteric experience, revelation is the exact contrary with numerous examples of prophets even making "an effort to escape such experience."[172]

This is where Heschel further develops his key assumption that it is God who looks out for the man and its successful encounter is what we can call revelation:

> Revelation is not the act of his [man's, AN] seeking, but of his being sought after, an act in God's search of man. [...] Seen from man's aspect, to receive revelation is *to witness how God is turning toward man.* [173]

As cited before, the Bible is *the report* of the revelation and for this the biblical text is considered a "litery fact, phrased in the language of man"[174]. Significant is therefore Heschel's consideration that revelation is not a monologue and ascribes to man an active partnership:

> In a sense, prophecy consists of a revelation of God and a co-revelation of man. The share of the prophet manifested itself not only in what he was able to give but also in what he was unable to receive. Revelation does not happen when God is alone. The two classical terms for the moment at Sinai are *mattan torah* and *kabbalat torah*, "the giving of the Torah" and "the acceptance of the Torah."[175]

To sum up, with Abraham Heschel we have a modern Jewish philosopher, who contributed in manifold ways to introduce a contemporary understanding of Orthodox Judaism for modern people; in order to do so, he discussed a model of understanding revelation and the Torah with a specific purpose. Indeed, he did not reduce the importance and authority of the biblical text by acknowledging a human contribution, but rather to stress the cultural, artificial nature of these traditional writings. His notions change to the anthropologic level and elevate the human to be the real addressee of the scripture by which the relevance of the content and the narratives is implied. On this subject, scholars[176] have noted how Heschel adopted Karl Barth's thoughts in formulation an anthropological turn. In *Das Word und die Theologie*

---

[172] Heschel 1956, 189

[173] Heschel 1956, 198

[174] Heschel 1956, 258

[175] Heschel 1956, 259–60

[176] Brill 2006, 3

(1928), Barth states: "It is not the right human thoughts about God which form the content of the Bible, but the right *divine thoughts* about men."[177]

5.3 Sommer's Argumentation Steps to a Participatory Revelation

After introducing the elements derived from exegetical work on the Sinai narrative in Exodus and some contributions from modern Jewish philosophy, this chapter is meant to illustrate the concept of participatory revelation based on the thought of Benjamin Sommer following three crucial arguments.

5.3.1 Minimalist and maximalist approaches of revelation

A first key aspect for discussing the question of a participated revelation is the extension of what has been directly revealed by God, what is assumed to be mediated and what is expected to be human. In fact, as Sommer shows that this distinction differs not only in postbiblical writings and Jewish thinkers of all ages but within the Books of the Pentateuch and redactions too. To help categorize the positions the terms *minimalist* and *maximalist approaches* are used. *Maximalist* indicates positions which assume that, at Sinai, the entire nation heard the words of the Decalogue while *minimalist* positions assume that all laws were mediated by Moses or by other human figures.[178]

According to Sommers's expositions[179], the four Torah sources (Elohist, Priestly, Jahwist and Deuteronomist) hold divergent positions on the nature of revelation. Among biblical scholars it is not clear if the Decalogue was part of the Elohist source, if it was added by a later redaction, or it was part of the Elohist source but implemented at a different section: Schwarz[180], following Wellhausen, assumes that the Decalogue, in an earlier version, was part of Elohist and – with the insertion of 19,20-25 which is attributed to the Jahwist source[181] – located between 19,19 und 20,18. Other scholars situate the Decalogue after the conversation between Moses and the people to join the

177 Brill 2006, 3 cites a translation of D. Horton (1957).

178 Sommer 2015, 75

179 Sommer 2015, 45–75

180 Schwarz 1997

181 Sommer 2015, 48 cites Schwarz 1997, 24–25

Decalogue with the Covenant laws[182], while a third group of scholar state that the Decalogue was not part of the Elohist document but was added in the redactional process of the Book Exodus.[183] These three options heavily influence the understanding of Elohist as a minimalist or maximalist position, indicating a stenographic or participatory understanding of revelation: 'E' without a Decalogue would mean that the people would not have heard the commandments with the consequence that all revealed content was mediated by Moses. In the case that the Decalogue was part of 'E', the result is much more ambiguous:

> An E that includes the Decalogue provides fodder to both a stenographic theory of revelation and a participatory theory as it problematizes both, but an E without a Decalogue leans more heavily in the direction of the participatory, since in that case the people can have heard the Decalogue only from Moses. [...] The authority of the specifics of the law has to rest on the reliability of Moses as an intermediary; the people have no way of knowing precisely what went on between Moses and the deity.[184]

For the priestly source, the extent in the Book of Exodus, look on a widespread agreement among scholars and includes, above that, the entire Book of Leviticus and Numbers (until 10,28)[185]. While the Elohist focuses more on the aspect of lawgiving and locates it at the event on Sinai, the priestly document proposes a different narrative: as Ex 24,15-17 shows, this source accurately describes God's presence as a manifestation in fire and covered by a cloud of smoke. Sommer[186] outlines how these elements are not a metaphoric or symbolical reference but expressions of God's presence. Typical for 'P' is the absence of storm-related language but, at the same time, an emphasis on "nonnarrative passages of considerable length that provide legal, ritual, sartorial, and architectural information".[187] Chapters 24-31 of Exodus present the detailed plan of God to build the tent where His Presence can dwell. In this tent, the law giving took place. There are mainly cultic and ritual laws and these are comprehended in large parts in the Book of Leviticus. Therefore, one main difference to 'E' is also the duration of the lawgiving: it largely paused for the period of 10 months

---

[182] This position is ascribed to a Dutch publication (1881) by Abraham Kuenen cited by Wellhausen (see footnote 83, Sommer 2015, 273).

[183] Sommer refers to „voluminous literature" on this position, among them the commentary of Noth 1962

[184] Sommer 2015, 49;50

[185] Sommer 2015, 53

[186] Sommer 2015, 55

[187] Sommer 2015, 54

since the Israelites arrived at Sinai (Ex 40,17), lasted for several weeks (Lev 11-25; 27), and reassumed again while the nation was crossing the wilderness (Num 35-36). In addition, all revelation in 'P' is mediated by Moses to the people or by him to Aaron or to/by Aaron's son, so that the nation heard the revealed content only through their human voices:

> [29]When Moses came down from Mount Sinai with the two tablets of the covenant law in his hands, he was not aware that his face was radiant because he had spoken with the Lord. [30]When Aaron and all the Israelites saw Moses, his face was radiant, and they were afraid to come near him. [31]But Moses called to them; so Aaron and all the leaders of the community came back to him, and he spoke to them. [32]Afterward all the Israelites came near him, and he gave them all the commands the Lord had given him on Mount Sinai. [33]When Moses finished speaking to them, he put a veil over his face. (Ex 34,29-33, NIV)

Accordingly, in the argumentation of Sommer, "P leans towards a participatory theology of revelation since the people receive all religious law through a human being rather than directly from God"[188].

The Jahwist source presents a similar approach to 'P' with an emphasis on visual aspects of revelation like fire and smoke. In contrast to 'E' and 'P', where the nation was frightened about these impressive events, the narration of 'J' depicts the revelation as something appealing to the people. For this, 'J' is associated with recurring warnings to Moses to not allow the nation to come close to or even in physical contact with him during the revelation as they would endanger themselves. Although the closeness between JHWH and His nation is central to 'J', this source shows a less "democratic" understanding of lawgiving involving presence of the people but at the same time highlighting the mediating role of Moses debunking a naïve understanding of a stenographic approach:

> J straightforwardly portrays access to the theophany as graduated. The whole nation witnesses Yhah's descent onto the top of the mountain, but from a distance; the people are not allowed to come close to the base of the mountain. [...] Moses alone approaches God [...] even he, however is unable to see the full manifestation of God's presence."[189]

[188] Sommer 2015, 59

[189] Sommer 2015, 62–63

The fourth source to be discussed is the Deuteronomist. This document represents a concise corpus of text, most of which can be found in the Book of Deuteronomy, can also be considered as the beginning of biblical commentary. In Sommer's words:

> These authors reformulate material found in earlier books of the Torah, and in doing so they clarify ambiguous statements, revise materials, and react to ideas the older sources express. [As a the oldest commentary], Exodus becomes Jewish scripture only in Deuteronomy, because Jews study scripture as Jews within a community of readers that include earlier Jews whose interpretation are available in classical commentaries.[190]

The redaction of the Deuteronomist source consists in clarifying ambiguities, emphasizing the verbal aspect rather than a cultic or visual one, providing justification for the reported laws[191], and pointing out how the lawgiving at Sinai was accessible to the present nation and not mediated:

The ambivalence of Exodus 19,16 and 20,18 with – *the voice* or *thunder* – *qol* [קוֹל] revisited in Dtn 4,12:

> [12]Then the Lord spoke to you out of the fire. You heard the sound of words but saw no form; there was only a voice. [NIV]

In this verse two key characteristic of 'D' can be identified: visual elements, which would lead towards a symbolic or cultic understanding, are rejected and replaced with the focus on verbal elements, which can be heard. The emphasis on the hearing is also restated in V.33 *Has any other people heard the voice of God speaking out of fire, as you have, and lived?* while P, J, and E feared to see God directly. Secondly, in this periscope, Israel is addressed directly as a nation; while the introduction to the Decalogue in Exodus reads *And God spoke all these words* (Ex 20,1; NIV), Deuteronomy is more explicit and states:

> [22]These are the commandments the Lord proclaimed in a loud voice to your whole assembly there on the mountain from out of the fire, the cloud and the deep darkness; and he added nothing more. (Dtn 5,22, NIV)

---

[190] Sommer 2015, 64

[191] Baden 2012, 130

The explanations regarding the addressees of the revelation and the concise nature imply that 'D' stands for a maximalist concept where the revelation of the Decalogue was addressed to the people and was heard without mediation.[192]

The dispute whether *qol* was a natural event or a voice perceptible to the human ear and whether the nation heard the Decalogue and other laws directly or through Mosaic and post-Mosaic mediation continues with post-biblical and medieval commentators. For the purpose of this thesis, I would like to elaborate on two positions:

The medieval commentators Rashbam (1085-1158) and Abraham Ibn Ezra (1089-1167) have a maximalist reading of the Decalogue and comment on Ex 20,27 where the nation, *after* they had heard the Decalogue, said to Moses *Then tell us,* which they interpreted as an indication that the other laws where mediated by Moses and for this the Decalogue stands out.[193] Some other sages, also from the Talmudic period, instead presented a minimalist reading, where only two out of the Ten Commandment where heard directly while others have been given by Moses. This is the case for the book Makkot of the Talmud, where the Rabbis Similai and Hamuna discuss the number of the commandments and state that 611 where given by Moses and two of them where commended by God: "Am I am Yhwh" and "You shall have no other gods".[194] We see how in order to amplify the authority for all 613 commandments, which are meant to be found in the Torah but have been listed in post-biblical writings, some thinkers had to minimize the amount of direct revelation to spread the authority to elements which were not explicitly located at Sinai.

According to Sommer, first elements for a theory of participatory revelation can be found in post-biblical commentators, but it has to kept in mind that "they do no articulate it fully"[195].

---

[192] Sommer 2015, 68

[193] Sommer 2015, 76 In fact, Sommer cites some Hebrew publication of Eran Viezel which, with a comprehensive look on further writings of Rashbam and Ibn Ezra, indicates how a maximalist, non-mediated understanding is only applicable for the Decalogue while the rest of the Torah is understood to have been mediated by human interaction.

[194] Sommer 2015, 77

[195] Sommer 2015, 80

5.3.2 Law and Commandment – A fruitful distinction

The second key argument towards a participatory revelation refers to a distinction between commandment and law. In this subchapter, the understanding of commandment as from divine and law from human origin, which is based on Rosenzweig's terms *Gebot* and *Gesetz,* will be introduced as well as some implications connected with it.

The differentiation between commandment (Gebot) and law (Gesetz) was originally articulated in Rosenzweig's *Star of Redemption*[196]. As we can recall from chapter 3.2.1, Rosenzweig points towards an existentialist understanding of revelation based on the self-disclosure of God with a focus on a super-linguistic communication. Accordingly, the revelation of God consists in commandments and not in specific laws. A commandment is characterized by immediacy, close relationship, and the lacking possibility to explain it through reason. Laws, on the contrary, are related to temporality and do not require an immediate presence.[197]

In this theoretical framework, Sommer articulates how the distinction between commandment and law can be applied to a Jewish understanding of participatory revelation:

> According to Rosenzweig's conception, the specifics of the law – that is, the actual legal directives found in the Pentateuch and in the rabbinic system of halakhah – do not come from God. They are rather interpretations of revelation to attempt to flesh out the prima command to love God. Divine command yields, but is not identical with, the laws authored by humans: the Jewish people transform *Gebot* into *Gesetz* – more precisely, into *Gesetze* (laws) in the plural.[198]

This adaptation of Rosenzweig's terminology is also forged by Heschel's view of the Torah as a human answer, a Midrash as divine revelation.[199] As a human response, the laws and the commandments are formulated by humans as an interpretation of God's will. The ultimate commands from God from which everything else follows "consist of a commanding presence and the call to love God"[200]. This assumption is

---

[196] Rosenzweig 1921

[197] Rosenzweig 1921, 197–99

[198] Sommer 2015, 118

[199] see Chapter 2.3.3; Heschel 1956, 185

[200] Sommer 2015, 118

based on what was articulated by Rosenzweig, who interprets the command *Love the Lord your God with all your heart and with all your soul and with all your strength. (Dtn, 6,5)* as the basis to understand what divine commands could mean[201], as well as on Heschel's view of revelation where the central point consists of God turning towards men.[202]

Nevertheless, the legal components of Jewish scripture and the aspect of legal obligation are essential for the Jewish religion. In the words of Sommer: "The response of the Jewish people to the revelation in Sinai, from biblical texts at least until the advent of modern era, have unanimously expressed themselves in terms of law"[203]. To distinguish therefore between *commandment* and *law* provides a theoretical basis to discuss the nature and authority of biblical and post-biblical legal systems but does not automatically override the observance of cultic or ethical-social laws in favour of a generic acceptance of divine command. In fact, without going too much into detail, even Heschel and Rosenzweig – of whom less traditional views on the observation of law would have been expected – assigned a crucial role to laws for the Jewish life and formulated a contemporary understanding for the observance of the law.[204]

For the purpose of this thesis, we might rather outline how the differentiation between commandment and law can contribute to a participatory understanding of biblical revelation. On the one side, it can help provide build a comprehensive framework for considering the plurality within the Torah and the biblical writings. If we take a concrete example of cultic laws regarding the preparations for Passover, one cannot ignore how contradictory and inconsistent the prescriptions are reported:

> Both Exodus 12 and Deuteronomy 16 require all Israelite families to slaughter and consume an animal as a Passover ritual. But they differ on details: Exodus 12.5 stipulates that the offering must be a lamb or a kid, while Deuteronomy 16.2 allows one to bring the offering from the flock or the herd [...] While Exodus 12.8 directs Israelites to roast the offering, Deuteronomy 16.6-7 require that the offering be boiled.[205]

---

[201] Rosenzweig 1921, 197 *Nur der Liebende, aber er auch wirklich, kann sprechen und spricht: Liebe mich. In seinem Munde ist das Gebot der Liebe kein fremdes Gebot, sondern nichts als die Stimme der Liebe selber. Die Liebe des Liebenden hat gar kein anderes Wort sich zu äußern als das Gebot. Alles andre ist schon nicht mehr unmittelbare Äußerung, sondern Erklärung – Liebes-erklärung.*

[202] Heschel 1951, 198

[203] Sommer 2015, 122

[204] Sommer 2015, 127–33

[205] Sommer 2015, 136–37

Sommer observes how for biblical and rabbinic text of all ages "a tactical flexibility regarding specific laws"[206] was permitted but, at the same time, the obedience to the legal system as an entity remains. Consequently, he traces an analogy and allocates the legal system as a whole to the commandment along with the more specific laws.[207] To differentiate between these two levels enables to contextualize biblical – and more important post-biblical – laws from a historical and critical perspective. The regression to the general divine commandment helps to distinguish between the "Torah's divine essence and the human particulars".[208]

5.3.3 Written Torah is Oral Torah

The third thesis to understand Sommer's approach towards a participated theology of revelation is probably the most ambitious one: If we assume that the Pentateuch is not a dictated and stenographically worded text, the distinction between *Oral* and *Written Torah* fades and "there is only *Oral Torah,* which starts with Genesis 1.1".[209] In order to understand the meaning of this differentiation, it is necessary to further deepen the knowledge on the concept of Written and Oral Torah so as to comprehend the impact of Sommer's thesis on (biblical) theology.

In Chapter 2.2[210], we already touched upon the distinction between Oral and Written Torah and understood how *Written Torah* does not only comprehend the Five Books of Moses but also the two other sections of the Tenak (the Prophets and the Writings), which constitute the canon of the Hebrew Bible. The *Oral Torah* refers to authoritative Rabbinic work, like the Talmud, which includes the Mishnah and Midrash, which were composed in the first centuries CE. Even if they are writings edited in books, the Torah is referred to as "oral" because of its dialogical and debating nature. On the contrary to what a Christian reader might assume, there is no distinctive primacy of the Written Torah over the "post-biblical" Oral Torah – the opposite is the case: For the Jewish life, for the study of the teaching and the practices of religion, the

[206] Sommer 2015, 137

[207] Sommer 2015, 136

[208] Sommer 2015, 138

[209] Sommer 2015, 147

[210] This paragraph partially recalls elements from Chapter 2.2. See the chapter for a better founded presentation.

Oral Torah is more relevant to be studied – with the consequence that the Written Torah was studied less due to an "efficiency" discourse:

> There is an agreement in principle that ideally a Jew should study both Written and Oral Torah (in particular the Pentateuch) and Oral Torah, but some authorities maintain that one can fulfil this dual obligation by studying Oral Torah alone. After all, rabbinic literature quotes scripture quite often, so by studying the rabies, one can kill two birds with one stone.[211]

The authority of the Oral Torah is also linked to the revelation at Sinai. In numerous Talmudic and Midrashic texts, the idea that Moses not only received the commandments and the laws reported in the books of the Pentateuch but also several which have been handed down orally and only in later times were composed into a text is articulated. Sommer notes that this maximalist approach – in the sense that all authoritative elements in Rabbinic Judaism are rooted in the Sinai revelation – increases over time.[212] An example from this later, *amoraic* period[213] in the Talmud shows these attempts to place all authoritative texts at the event of the revelation at Sinai. In commenting Exodus 24,12 *The Lord said to Moses, "Come up to me on the mountain and stay here, and I will give you the tablets of stone with the law and commandments I have written for their instruction"*. Rabbi levi bar Hama said:

> What is the meaning of the verse: And I will give thee the tables of stone, and the law and the commandment, which I have written that thou mayest teach them? 'Tables of stone': these are the ten commandments; 'the law': this is the Pentateuch; 'the commandment': this is the Mishnah; 'which I have written': these are the Prophets and the Hagiographa; 'that thou mayest teach them': this is the Gemara. It teaches [us] that all these things were given to Moses on Sinai.[214]

The Oral Torah was further extended by some aggadic[215] commentaries to not only comprehend the Mishnah and Gemara but also the oral discussions, which continue until today:

> The midrash from Shemot Rabbah 41:1 tells us that the revealed Torah includes questions students would one day ask their masters. Other versions of the text [...] tell us that what keen-witted students would one

[211] Sommer 2015, 153

[212] Sommer 2015, 150

[213] Amoraic refers to the period of Sages between 200-500 CE. The Sages from the earlier period (0-200) are refered to as Tannaim.

[214] Talmud b. Berakhot 5a retrieved from Sommer 2015, 152

[215] Aggadic refers to the non-legalistic exegisis of biblical texts. See Chapter 2.1

> day teach in the presence of their masters is also part of the revealed Torah. Oral Torah includes the living words of students in every generation.[216]

We can conclude that not only is the Oral Torah more relevant in shaping and ruling the religious life, its authority is neither reduced by the fact that it is based on human formulation nor by the diversity of opinions contained. Moreover, if we consider the Written Torah in the context of the Oral Torah, a new dimension is taken into account: For its dialogic nature, the Oral Torah is meant to be discussed for its commentaries and sayings of the sages, analyzed, disputed and further commented. Therefore, if we adopt this approach to the written text new, opportunities arise for the handling of scripture. Nevertheless, embracing an understanding of participatory revelation does not mean to deny the divine origin of the commandments entailed in the text but "merely pushes the heavenly origin back by a single step. Instead of an earthly Talmudic law based on a heavenly Pentateuch, the participatory theory yields an earthly Talmudic law based on an earthly Pentateuch that in its turn based on a heavenly, albeit nonverbal command."[217]

---

[216] Sommer 2015, 156

[217] Sommer 2015, 187

6 Das katholische Lehramt: Dei Verbum

Folgendes Kapitel stellt den Übergang von der Darstellung eines jüdischen Offenbarungsverständnisses zum Vergleich mit dem christlich-katholischem Verständnis her. Dabei soll die dogmatische Konstitution Dei Verbum die höchste Autoritätscussage zum Veständnis von Offenbarung einen möglichst relevanten Vergleich möglich machen. Schon aus der Darstellung wird ersichtlich, wie einige der Themen, die in der jüdischen Ausführung gefallen sind – so etwa der Aspekt der Selbstoffenbarung und die Weitung des Offenbarungverständnisses auf nonverbale Aspekte – bereits im Zweiten Vatikanum gefallen sind.

Als Übergang zum Diskussionsteil dieser Arbeit soll in diesem Kapitel die Position des katholischen Lehramtes[218] angerissen werden. Dafür wurde die *Dogmatische Konstitution über die göttliche Offenbarung – Dei Verbum*[219] herangezogen, da diese sich inhaltlich sehr gut an die Darstellung von Sommer anfügt und zugleich als Dokument aus dem Zweiten Vatikanischen Konzil die gegenwertig höchste lehramtliche Autoritätsaussage vertritt.

Der Weg zum promulgierten Text von *Dei Verbum* war ein sehr langer: Schon Mitte November 1962 wurden den Konzilsvätern erste Schemata vorgelegt, die jedoch sehr kritisch diskutiert und zu einem großen Teil abgelehnt wurden. Es waren mehrere Sitzungsperioden und Neubestellungen der Kommissionen, die am Dokument gearbeitet hatten, notwendig, so dass erst in der dritten Sitzungsperiode im Jahr 1965 die Endfassung breite Zustimmung fand.[220] Besonders intensiv wurden die Fragen zur Irrtumslosigkeit der Schrift und zur Historizität diskutiert sowie Themen zum Verhältnis von Schrift und Tradition.[221] Spezifische Änderungsvorschläge an Kapiteln der Konstitution wurden sowohl von Papst Paul VI. wie vom österreichischen Kardinal Franz König, der sich als habilitierter Bibelwissenschaftler gerade den Aspekt der Möglichkeit, dass der biblische Text Irrtümer enthalten könne, hinein reklamieren.[222] Die vierte Fassung der Konstitution wurde mit der Übernahme einiger Änderungen am

[218] Es wurde bewusst versucht, die katholische Position als Vergleichsgegenstand nicht über Publikationen einzelner katholischer TheologInnen aufzustellen, sondern gerade über die Konsenslage der höchsten dogmatischen Formulierungen wie eben jene eines Konzilsdokumentes.

[219] Zweites Vatikanisches Konzil 1965, Im weiteren Verlauf werden wörtliche Zitate mit Anführungszeichen wiedergegeben und mit dem Dokumentenkürzel DV und der entsprechenden Artikelnummer zitiert.

[220] Rahner und Vorgrimler 1990, 361

[221] Kirchschläger 1985, 5–6

[222] Kirchschläger 2014, 115 siehe die *Rede von Kardinal König am 2. Oktober 1964 bei der 93. Generalkongregation.*

29. Oktober 1965 mit 2.081 *placet*, 27 non *placet* und einem *placet iuxta modum* von den Konzilsvätern angenommen und am 18. November 1965 feierlich proklamiert.

Im Folgenden soll dieses lehramtliche Dokument in einer Übersicht präsentiert werden, fokussiert auf vier Leitthesen, die dem Dokument zugrunde liegen und in Hinblick auf die thematische Ausrichtung dieser Arbeit formuliert wurden. Hinweise aus einschlägigen Kommentaren sollen helfen, die Dynamik der Formulierungen gerade in Bezug auf Streitpositionen in den letzten Konzilen der Kirchengeschichte nachzuvollziehen.

6.1 Offenbarung ist Dialog

Im ersten Kapitel skizziert *Dei Verbum* die Eigenschaften von Offenbarung und wie in diesem Dokument und im kirchlichen Lehramt von Offenbarung gesprochen werden kann. Schon der erste Satz drückt deutlich aus, wie die Offenbarung Gottes in erster Linie als Selbstoffenbarung verstanden werden muss: „Gott hat in seiner Güte und Weisheit beschlossen, sich selbst zu offenbaren und das Geheimnis seines Willens kundzutun" (DV 2). Die Selbstzugabe Gottes ist zudem ganz auf einer innigen Beziehungsebene gedacht, wo Gott „aus überstrebender Liebe die Menschen wie Freunde" anspricht, mit „ihnen verkehrt" und sie „in seine Gemeinschaft" einlädt und aufnimmt (DV 2). Das Offenbarungsgeschehen ist keine rein unidirektionale Mitteilung, sondern im hohen Maße über Menschen vermittelt und auf die Antwort der Menschen ausgerichtet. Dieses geschah als „Gott viele Male und auf viele Weisen durch die Propheten gesprochen hatte" (DV 4) und dann, in Jesus Christus als „fleischgewordenes Wort", heilsgeschichtlich überholt wurde, wo er als „Mensch zu den Menschen" (DV 4) gesprochen hatte. Dieses Motiv wird an einer späteren Stelle wiederholt:

> Denn Gottes Worte, durch Menschenzunge formuliert, sind menschlicher Rede ähnlich geworden, wie einst des ewigen Vaters Wort durch die Annahme menschlich-schwachen Fleisches den Menschen ähnlich geworden ist. (DV 13)

Die Form des Dialoges sieht auch eine „Antwort" des Gesprächspartners vor, die hier eben von den Menschen als eine Zustimmung im Glauben[223] verstanden wird:

[223] Eigentlich „Gehorsam des Glaubens" [oboeditio fidei], was auf die Formulierung in 2 Kor 10,6 zurückzuführen ist.

„Darin überantwortet sich der Mensch Gott als ganzer in Freiheit, indem er sich ‚dem offenbarenden Gott mit Verstand und Wille voll unterwirft' und seiner Offenbarung willig zustimmt" (DV 5).

Was in Kommentaren deutlich hervorgeht, ist die Betonung des dialogischen Beziehungscharakters[224], der hier grundgelegt wird. Diese Auffassung steht in Ergänzung zu den Formulierungen des Konzils von Trient (1545-1563) und jenen des Ersten Vaticanums (1869-1870), welche Offenbarung eher „intellektualistisch als bloße Mitteilung von Sätzen ‚über' Gott und seine Heilsabsichten"[225] gedacht hatten.

6.2 Offenbarung ist Weitergabe

Durch den Beziehungscharakter ist die Partizipation der Menschen an der Formulierung, Vermittlung und Weitergabe [transmissione] des Offenbarungsgeschehens grundgelegt. Zwar ist die Offenbarung in und durch Christus vollendet (DV 2, 4, 7) jedoch kam den Menschen, insbesondere den Aposteln, eine wichtige Aufgabe zu, damit das, „was Gott zum Heil aller Völker geoffenbart hatte [...] für alle Zeiten unversehrt erhalten bleibe und allen Geschlechtern weitergegeben werde." (DV 7) Trotz der Betonung der Begrifflichkeiten, wie Treue, Unversehrtheit, Zuverlässigkeit oder Wahrheit in diesen und weiteren Artikeln, tritt *Dei Verbum* nicht für ein Verständnis ein, wo Wortgenau eine akustische Offenbarung zu Text gemacht wurde, sondern beschreibt gerade eine teilnehmende Rolle der Menschen in der Nachfolge Christi:

> Darum hat Christus der Herr [...] den Aposteln geboten, das Evangelium, das er als die Erfüllung der früher ergangenen prophetischen Verheißung selbst gebracht und persönlich öffentlich verkündet hat, allen zu predigen als die Quelle jeglicher Heilswahrheit und Sittenlehre und ihnen so göttliche Gaben mitzuteilen. Das ist treu ausgeführt worden, und zwar sowohl durch die Apostel, die durch mündliche Predigt, durch Beispiel und Einrichtungen weitergaben, was sie aus Christi Mund, im Umgang mit ihm und durch seine Werke empfangen oder was sie unter der Eingebung des Heiligen Geistes gelernt hatten, als auch durch jene Apostel und apostolischen Männer, die unter der Inspiration des gleichen Heiligen Geistes die Botschaft vom Heil niederschrieben. (DV 7)

[224] Kirchschläger 1985, 11

[225] Rahner und Vorgrimler 1990, 362

In diesem Textauszug werden zahlreiche Themen angerissen: Zum einen wird auf das Predigen, auf eine mündliche Sprachform eingegangen, die eben gerade nicht für ein Verständnis von bloßer Replizierung von auditiven Offenbarungswahrnehmungen stehen kann, sondern für eine engagierte Art der Vermittlung von Offenbarungsinhalten. Zum anderen kommt aus dem Text hervor, wie die Kulminierung der Offenbarung in Christus sich nicht nur auf verbale Komponenten beschränkte, sondern dass ebenso (und gleichwertig) auch non-verbale Dimensionen zum Offenbarungsgeschehen gezählt werden. Darüber zeichnet sich ein Parallelismus ab, zwischen der Form der Offenbarung durch Christi und der Verkündigung der Aposteln und der apostolischen Männer: Die Predigt [praedicatione orali] steht in der Promulgation von dem was aus "Christi Mund" [ex ore] gesprochen wurde. Das was durch Beispiel [exemplis] weitergegeben wird, steht parallel zu "Umgang mit ihm" [conversatione]. Die Einrichtungen [institutiones] können im nächsten Satz auf die Werke Christi [operibus Christi] zurückgeführt werden.

Im eröffnenden Artikel des 2. Kapitels klingt auch an, wie die Eingebung [inspiratione] durch den Heiligen Geist am Entstehungsprozess des Verfassungsvorganges beteiligt sei. Dieses Mitwirken des Heiligen Geistes beschränkt sich jedoch nicht nur auf das Verfassen der Heiligen Schriften (vgl. auch DV 11), sondern trägt dazu bei, dass von einem Fortschritt in der apostolischen Überlieferung gesprochen werden kann. Obwohl an mehreren Stellen die Abgeschlossenheit der Offenbarung in Christus betont wird, wird eine Annahme von Weiterentwicklung und Wachstum für die apostolische Überlieferung nicht ausgeschlossen:

> Es wächst das Verständnis der überlieferten Dinge und Worte durch das Nachsinnen und Studium der Gläubigen, die sie in ihrem Herzen erwägen, durch innere Einsicht, die aus geistlicher Erfahrung stammt, durch die Verkündigung derer, die mit der Nachfolge im Bischofsamt das sichere Charisma der Wahrheit empfangen haben; denn die Kirche strebt im Gang der Jahrhunderte ständig der Fülle der göttlichen Wahrheit entgegen, bis an ihr sich Gottes Worte erfüllen. (DV 8)

Blum spricht von einem „ganzheitlichen und dynamischen Traditionsbegriff in Dei Verbum"[226], welcher aufgrund der komplexen Natur der weiterzugebenden Inhalte des Evangeliums gerade aus einem Zusammenspiel aus schriftlichen und nicht-schriftlichen Überlieferungen konstituiert wird.

[226] Blum 1971, 43

Weitere Überlegungen zu der Frage des Wachstums der Überlieferung werden in Abschnitt 6.4 folgen.

6.3 Doppelte Autorenschaft und menschliche Irrtümer

Mitunter die brisanteste und für das Thema dieser Arbeit zentralste Frage wird im Artikel 11 angerissen. Es wird festgestellt, dass alle kanonischen Bücher, sowohl jene des Alten wie des Neuen Testamentes, „Gott zum Urheber haben“ und Menschen sie „als echte Verfasser schriftlich“ (DV 11) überlieferten. Der Blick ins lateinische Original verrät, dass für beide Begriffe *auctorem* bzw. *auctores* verwendet wird. Zusätzlich wird auch skizziert, wie die auserwählten Menschen „durch den Gebrauch der eigenen Fähigkeiten und Kräfte“ (DV 11) Gott bei der Abfassung der Heiligen Schrift dienen sollen. Auch in Artikel 12 wird deutlich, wie die Schrift eindeutig eine menschliche Komponente anführt, da „Gott in der Heiligen Schrift durch Menschen nach Menschenart gesprochen hat“ (DV 12), die entsprechend auch historisch und kulturell bestimmt ist. Explizit wird erwähnt, wie die literarische Gattung die Darstellung und den Aussagemodus eines Textes jeweils beeinflussen kann: „Denn die Wahrheit wird je anders dargelegt und ausgedrückt in Texten von in verschiedenem Sinn geschichtlicher, prophetischer oder dichterischer Art, oder in anderen Redegattungen“ (DV 12). Auch für kulturhistorische Aspekte, die eben durch die menschliche Dimension der Heiligen Schrift Eintritt finden, bleibt nicht unausgesprochen, wo Zeit und Umwelt der Verfasser die „damals im Alltagsverkehr üblichen“ Sprach- und Erzählformen beeinflusst hat. Daher betont dieser Artikel mehrmals wie „der Schrifterklärer [interpres Sacrae Scripturae]” sorgfältig forschen muss [attente investigare debet], “um zu erfassen, was Gott uns mitteilen wollte, […] was die heiligen Schriftsteller wirklich zu sagen beabsichtigten und was Gott mit ihren Worten kundtun wollte.” (DV 12)

In der Rezeption von *Dei Verbum* wird der Frage nach der Autorenschaft besonders viel Aufmerksamkeit gewidmet: Seit dem Konzil von Trient, so auch im Ersten Vaticanum, wurde die Urheberschaft Gottes als Autor hervorgehoben; diese lehramtliche Aussage wird erweitert, indem auch die Menschen in das „Autorenteam“ geholt werden.[227] Es geht eben gerade darum, die Menschen nicht als bloße

[227] Vgl. Kirchschläger 2014, 144

Stenographen oder Sekretäre eines göttlichen Diktates zu sehen, sondern gerade um die Beteiligung als echte Verfasser [veri auctores].[228] Kirchschläger hebt auch hervor, wie der Verweis der Beruf dieser Menschen, mit ihren Fähigkeiten und Kräften, auch bedeutet, dass er mit den Menschen ein Risiko eingeht, „wenn sie die biblischen Texte schreiben“[229] und zum anderen, dass mit den Fähigkeiten und Kräften diese berufene Menschen eben auch ihre menschliche Schwächen und Fehler in den Verfassungsprozess mitnehmen.[230]

Diese Fehler werden gerade für die Schriften des Alten Testamentes eingeräumt: „Obgleich diese Bücher auch Unvollkommenes [imperfecta] und Zeitbedingtes [temporanea] enthalten, zeigen sie doch eine wahre göttliche Erziehungskunst“ (DV 15). Dieser Gedanke wurde schon von Papst Pius XXI. in der Enzyklika *Mit brennender Sorge* (1937) formuliert, wo – obwohl es darum geht, gerade auch den konstituierenden Beitrag der alttestamentlichen Schriften für den christlichen hervor zu heben – diese vor allem aufgrund der menschlichen Komponenten als stark defizitär dargestellt werden:

> Wie es bei Geschichts- und Gesetzbüchern nicht anders sein kann, sind sie in manchen Einzelheiten ein Spiegelbild menschlicher Unvollkommenheit, Schwäche und Sünde. Neben unendlich vielem Hohen und Edlen erzählen sie auch von der Veräußerlichung und Verweltlichung, die in dem die Offenbarung und die Verheißungen Gottes tragenden alttestamentlichen Bundesvolk immer wieder hervorbrachen. Für jedes nicht durch Vorurteil und Leidenschaft geblendete Auge leuchtet jedoch aus dem menschlichen Versagen, von dem die biblische Geschichte berichtet, um so strahlender das Gotteslicht der über alle Fehde und Sünde letztlich triumphierenden Heilsführung hervor.[231]

In einer Rede bei der Diskussion der Schemata der Textes setzte Kardinal König einen wegweisenden Akzent, dass beim Zweiten Vatikanischen Konzil nicht weiter blind an der Irrtumslosigkeit der Heiligen Schrift festzuhalten sei. Er nennt dabei historische Ungenauigkeiten, bspw. Fehler in der Datierung von alttestamentlichen Königsfiguren sowie falsche Zuschreibungen von Schriftzitaten in den Evangelien.[232]

---

[228] Rahner und Vorgrimler 1990, 363

[229] Kirchschläger 2014, 144

[230] Kirchschläger 1985, 27

[231] Pius XI. 1937, Artikel 19

[232] Kirchschläger 2014, 111 zitiert dabei die Rede von Franz König an der 93. Generalkongregation des Zweiten Vatikanischen Konzils am 2. Oktober 1964.

Der Einbezug der menschlichen Partizipation im Abfassungsprozess und der, an manchen Stellen ungenauen oder widersprüchlichen Darstellung der Inhalte, machen es möglich, die Wahrheitsgehalte und die Autorität des Wortes Gottes hochzuhalten und vor vereinfachenden Anfechtungen zu retten. So rekonstruiert Kirchschläger wie der Tenor, in dem *Dei Verbum* diesen Aspekt der Frage zur Irrtumslosigkeit der Schrift behandelt, auf das Motiv der doppelten Autorenschaft zurückgeführt wird. Diese Schwerpunktsetzung wurde von Kardinal König maßgeblich mitverantwortet und kann in seiner schon angeführten Rede herausgelesen werden.

> So ist, damit die Autorität der Heiligen Schrift keinen Schaden leidet, ernst und ohne Zweideutigkeit zu sprechen, nicht künstlich und mit Furcht: d.h., dass die Kenntnis des Verfassers im Hinblick auf historische Angaben gemäß den Umständen seiner Zeit begrenzt gewesen ist und daß Gott ihn als solchen zum Schreiben bewegt hat. Wenn wir so die Herablassung des göttlichen Wortes, das menschlicher Rede ähnlich ist, bekräftigen, dann verteidigen wir besser Gottes Wort im Menschenwort.[233]

6.4 Schrift und Tradition – eine oder zwei Quellen?

Das vierte große Thema, das von *Dei Verbum* grundgelegt wird, ist das Verhältnis von Schrift und Tradition. In diesem Abschnitt soll gerade auf die Annahme eines gemeinsamen Ursprunges eingegangen werden. Artikel 9 unterstreicht wie die „Heilige Überlieferung [Traditio] und die Heilige Schrift [Scriptura] eng miteinander verbunden sind“ (DV 9), gerade weil sie am selben Anteil haben. Es wird im Singular von demselben göttlichen Quell [ex eadem divina scaturigine] gesprochen, aus dem beide entspringen und einem gemeinsam Ziel zuströmen. Die stark bildliche Sprache wird durch kurze Erklärungen ergänzt, wo die Schrift als Gottes Rede bezeichnet wird, „insofern sie unter dem Anhauch des Heiligen Geistes schriftlich aufgezeichnet wurde“ (DV 9). Die Heilige Überlieferung, die kirchliche Tradition, trägt sehr ähnliche Charakteristika, als sie „das Wort Gottes, das von Christus dem Herrn und vom Heiligen Geist den Aposteln anvertraut wurde, unversehrt an deren Nachfolger“ weitergibt und „unter der erleuchtenden Führung des Geistes der Wahrheit in ihrer Verkündigung treu“ bewährt, erklärt und ausbreitet [fideliter servent, exponant atque diffundant].

[233] Kirchschläger 2014, 112; siehe Anmerkung oben.

Die Heilige Schrift alleine genügt im katholischen Lehramt nicht, um die Offenbarung Gottes in seiner Totalität zu erhalten, denn es ist eine „Fortführung des Textes“[234] durch das Wirken des Heiligen Geistes in der Kirche mitgedacht. Gerade auch die Schlussbemerkung des Artikels, „Daher sollen beide mit gleicher Liebe und Achtung [pari pietatis affectu ac reverential] angenommen und verehrt werden“ (DV 9), zeigt, wie beide Ströme einander zugeordnet sind und nicht gegeneinander ausgespielt werden sollen.[235] Durch das Bild der einen Quelle wird auch vermieden, die Tradition als eine „quantitative materiale Ergänzung der Schrift“ zu verstehen, sondern durch die Betonung der Einheit, den Aspekt der Weitergabe, die einen Fortschritt qualitativer Art, im Sinne eines je tieferen Verständnisses, vollzieht.[236]

---

[234] Kirchschläger 1985, 23

[235] ebd.

[236] Rahner und Vorgrimler 1990, 363

7 Diskussion

Nach der Darstellung der Zugänge aus jüdischer und christlich-katholischer Seite soll nun im Diskussionsteil der Vergleich und die Synthese angegangen werden. Im ersten Unterpunkt sollen die Grenzen und Möglichkeiten des Vergleichs aufgezeigt sowie gerade auf die Chancen geblickt werden, die daraus entstehen können. In Unterpunkt darauf wird ausgehend von den Befunden der Arbeit das Thema des Schriftverständnisses angerissen, in dem auch einzelne überkonfessionelle Überlegungen thematisiert gehören. Im Anschluss werden aus den Überlegungen erste Schlüsse für theologische Forschungspraxis und Pastoral gezogen.

7.1 Judentum und Lehramt: Zur Frage der Vergleichbarkeit

Bei der Darstellung vom Konzept der partizipierten Offenbarung handelte es sich nicht um eine historisch-systematische Aufarbeitung eines Konzeptes, sondern um die Besprechung einer zeitgenössischen wissenschaftlichen Publikation eines jüdischen Theologen mit der Gegenüberstellung eines dogmatischen Dokumentes aus dem katholischen Lehramt. Ein solch exemplarisches Vorgehen ist nicht zuletzt dem geschuldet, dass das Konzept einer partizipierten Offenbarung in vielen Schriften entweder nur implizit, oder unter anderen Vorzeichen angegangen wird, oder eben in vielen Forschungstraditionen noch keinen Eingang gefunden hat. Nicht zuletzt soll es auch darum ein Anliegen sein, mit einer Diskussion zu den Grenzen der Vergleichbarkeit zu beginnen, um dann differenziert auf Überlegungen über zu gehen, in denen die Möglichkeiten und gegenseitige Befruchtungen aufgezeigt werden, die einer solchen Synopse entspringen können.

Als erstes muss angemerkt werden, wie „das“ Judentum und der Katholizismus unterschiedliche „theologische Architekturen“ aufweisen, die einen Vergleich fragwürdig machen. Während das katholische Lehramt nicht nur einen systematischen Korpus an Lehrdokumenten, ein geregeltes System für die Weiterentwicklung und Definition autoritativer Texte und eine zentrale Hierarchie zur Steuerung aufweisen, ist das Judentum weitaus dezentraler organisiert. Dies schlägt sich nicht zuletzt auch darin aus, dass die Auslegungshoheit nicht an übergreifende Instanzen gebunden ist, sondern dass je nach Rabbi, je nach Synagoge, Unterschiede anzutreffen sind, die für eine spürbare Pluralität stehen. Dieser, an Vielfalt orientierter, Zugang reicht von der

Struktur der rabbinischen Texte, über traditionelle Schriftdidaktik (Chavrusa)[237], in der es um eine aktive Diskussion und Auseinandersetzung mit Argumenten und Schriftstellen geht, bis hin zu der sozial-religiösen Ordnungsgewalt, die dem Rabbi vor Ort und nicht einem übergeordneten Rabbinat zukommt[238].

Intuitiv würde man meinen, dass zumindest das Alte Testament jene gemeinsame Basis bildet, die einen Vergleich möglich macht. Aber auch dieser Aspekt soll – trotzt dem meist selben Wortlaut der biblischen Schriften - nicht überstrapaziert werden: Obwohl alle Bücher der hebräischen Bibel im christlichen Kanon enthalten sind, drückt die unterschiedliche Anordnung und die Aufteilung des Kanons, neben dem Einbezug weiterer Bücher, auch ein andersgeartetes theologisches Programm aus.[239] Auch die anders ausfallende Relevanz einzelner Schriften, etwa die Auslegung der großen Propheten/Hinteren Propheten im Christentum, geben der Frage Nachdruck, wie stark die geteilten Bibelschriften Gemeinsamkeit und Vergleichbarkeit von Judentum und Christentum ausdrücken. Dies trifft gerade auf die kultischen Gesetze der Priesterschrift zu, die mitunter die größte Diskrepanz im Verständnis und in der religiösen Praxis zwischen Juden und Christen ausmachen[240], wo jedoch die Beachtung der *mitzvot* – was sich auch in der Ausrichtung der Argumentation von Sommer zeigte – Hauptreferenzpunkt in der jüdischen Glaubenspraxis darstellt. Damit verbunden ist auch die teilweise vollkommene Ahnungslosigkeit von Seite des Christentums über die Inhalte und Funktionen der rabbinischen Literatur, die den Dialog und eine gegenseitige Rezeption unmöglich macht.

Daher ist gerade die Auseinandersetzung mit dem Judentum, im Studium sowie in der Vermittlung, Ausgangspunkte nicht nur des Dialoges sondern über das Lernen an Gemeinsamkeiten und Unterschiede, auch Quelle der theologischen Reflexion der

---

[237] Kent and Cook 2014 und Mirvis 2012 zeigen auf, wie die traditionelle Methode der Chavrusa (חַבְרוּתָא) für das biblische und schulische Lernen neu entdeckt werden soll, wo das Lernen mit den Schriften nicht in Einzel-, sondern im Partnerarbeit im Dialog stattfindet, wo die Positionen logisch stringent definiert werden, um dann vom Partner angefochten zu werden, um sie anschließend treffender zu formulieren, mit dem Ziel, dass beide zu einem tieferen Verständnis gelangen. Diese Lernmethode wird mit Zitaten aus dem Talmud belegt, wie Berachot 63a: „Indeed, the Talmud goes so far as to say that one who learns Torah alone becomes foolish." oder Shabbat 63a: „When two scholars of Torah listen to one another, God hears their voices" (zit. nach Mirvis 2012).

[238] In den letzten Jahren werden etwa die Kritiken rund um die hegemonische Stellung des Jerusalemer Großrabbinats immer lauter, die gerade die dezentralisierte Autorität der Rabbiner in den Synagogen vor Ort als dem Judentum eigentümlichem Modell wieder einfordern. Siehe etwa Golnik 2013 oder Farber 2018

[239] vgl. Kapitel 4.3

[240] Zenger 2008, 175

eigenen Tradition. Im Schreibprozess des jüdischen Teils dieser Arbeit stellte es sich manchmal als schwierig heraus, sich zurückzuhalten, erste Assoziationen und vielleicht noch voreilige Vergleiche in Fußnoten zu vermerken, da diese an vielen Stellen spontan aufkamen. Allein die Tatsache, dass es einen gemeinsamen Ursprung gibt, bzw. sich das Christentum aus einer Reformbewegung des Rabbinischen Judentum herauslöste und sich eigenständig über Jahrhunderte weiterentwickelte, macht es wenig verwunderlich, dass Gelegenheiten, einen Vergleich zu ziehen, so schnell auskamen. So ist es gerade das Ziel und das Produkt eines solchen Vergleiches, neue Schlaglichter auf die eigene theologische Entwicklung zu werfen, um im Anschluss die Modifikationen und die Parallelitäten in den inhaltlichen Entwicklungen aufzuzeigen. Gerade an den Biographien der in der Arbeit vorgestellten Philosophen[241] wird ersichtlich, wie die Trennungslinien zwischen Judentum und Christentum sehr subjektiv verlaufen und wie die Rezeption von Denkmodellen, die in der christlichen Umwelt geprägt wurden, so stark im Vordergrund steht. Mit Blick auf die Auseinandersetzung mit Rosenzweig bringt Rutishauser den Dialog zwischen Judentum und Christentum folgendermaßen auf den Punkt: „Die An- und Abgrenzung beider Glaubensgemeinschaften dürfte viel komplexer, paradoxer und geheimnisvoller sein"[242]. Vor allem für die katholische Theologie kann dies ein ganz besonderer Moment sein, dort wo Elemente der christlichen bzw. christlich geprägten Tradition durch jüdische Denker aufgearbeitet und der christlichen Tradition wieder zurückgespielt werden. So würden manche Aspekte in *Dei Verbum* einer weiterführenden und vertieften Analyse bedürfen, welche etwa aufarbeiten könnte, wie die Frage nach der Betonung der Zentralität der Selbstoffenbarung und Beziehungsdimension Gottes nicht zuletzt womöglich auf die Kenntnis der Konzilsväter der Schriften von Buber und Rosenzweig zurückzuführen sind, wo die Konzile zuvor eher die intellektualistischen Dimensionen der göttlichen Offenbarung in den Mittelpunkt stellten.[243]

Die ertragreichste Möglichkeit für die katholische Theologie stellen jedoch der jüdische Blick auf das Alte Testament und damit insbesondere der Fokus auf die exegetischen Betrachtungen dar. Der Glaubensdifferenz geschuldet muss sich das

[241] vgl. Kapitel 5.2

[242] Rutishauser 2016, 134

[243] vgl. Kapitel 6.1

katholische Lehramt an dem Christusereignis und dessen soteriologische Zentralität orientieren, um so auch mit den weiteren christlichen Denominationen anschlussfähig zu bleiben. Jedoch meine ich, dass der Christusglaube nicht (mehr) der apologetischen Diskreditierung des Alten Testamentes bedarf und eine konstitutive Neubewertung der alttestamentlichen Schriften – gerade auch jenseits der Ankündigungslogik – vollziehen kann und das Alte Testament und die Kommunikation Gottes mit dem Volk Israel, mit der Menschheit, in den Mittelpunkt der offenbarungstheologische Debatten rückt. Blicken wir dabei auch auf die Argumentationsstruktur von *Dei Verbum,* sehen wir, wie textimmanente und exegetische Argumentationslinien gänzlich fehlen, oder am ehesten implizit in der Diskursanalyse[244] zu erkennen sind. Die Arbeit von Sommer und gerade seine ausführlichen exegetischen Betrachtungen zeigen, wie die wissenschaftliche Auseinandersetzung mit der Schrift selbst, noch vor dem Einbezug philosophischer Denkmodelle und lehramtlichen Entwicklungen, theologisches Innovationspotential hervorbringt und wie ein Konzept der partizipierten Offenbarung kein moderner Zugang ist, sondern so in der Vielschichtigkeit des Pentateuchs schon mit grundgelegt ist. Klarerweise erfordert ein solcher textimmanenter Bezog jedoch ein Verständnis von Schrift, das durch die Historizität von Pluralität und Diskursen geprägt und geformt worden ist, wodurch erst ein kritischer Vergleich aufgrund von bibelwissenschaftlichen Entstehungshypothesen möglich wird.

7.2 Sola Scriptura? Auslegung und Schriftverständnis

Die Auseinandersetzung mit dem Themenbereich dieser Arbeit führte nicht nur entlang der Linien des jüdisch-christlichen Dialogs, sondern wirft gerade auch Schatten auf das Verhältnis im Schriftverständnis der katholischen Kirche mit den reformierten Traditionen. So sehr starke Gemeinsamkeiten in der Komplementarität von Bibel und nachbiblischen, religiösen Schriften zwischen Judentum und Katholizismus gefunden werden, gerade im Bezug der Lehre von Interdependenz[245] und der Ablehnung, die Bibel für sich stehend zu lesen, stellten sich aber gerade Differenzlinien zwischen diesen Traditionen und den reformierten Kirchen. Dies trifft gerade auf das Schriftverständnis zu, das in der Theologiegeschichte auch das

[244] vgl. etwa den Beitrag von König bei der Diskussion der Textentwurfes, der sowohl von Forschungsergebnissen aus der Orientalistik wie aus eigenen exegetischen Arbeiten berichtet, um für Änderungen am Konzilsdokument zu argumentieren. Kirchschläger 2014, 112

[245] Dieser Aspekt musste in der Arbeit teilweise ausgelassen werden, siehe aber Sommer 2015, 147ff

Verhältnis von Judentum und Christentum stark belastet hat.[246] Aber gerade das Verständnis von Schrift scheint hierbei schon ein erstes Dilemma zu generieren, dass in dieser Diskussion behandelt werden soll:

Durch die Ablehnung von kirchlichen Lehrdokument, die als menschliches Werk die dem Wort Gottes gegenüberstehen, wird die Schrift hochstilisiert zur einzigen Quelle der Lehre, die „in Bezeugung ihrer Sache (Christus) klar ist [...] keiner Interpretation [bedürfe] und selbst das Licht [ist] das Menschenworte erleuchtet. [...]“[247]. Diese Auffassung wurde dann als *sola scriptura* zum Eckstein der reformierten Theologie, die programmatisch nur mit den Texten der Heiligen Schrift (im Kanon der Lutherbibel) auskommt. Obwohl in den Anfängen der Reformation, so auch bei Luther und Melanchthon, der vierfache Schriftsinn abgelehnt wurde zugunsten einer Beschränkung der Exegese auf den Literalsinn[248], entwickelten sich historisch-kritische Methoden vordergründig im protestantischen Bereich. Zugänge, welche archäologisches und sprachwissenschaftliches Repertoire in die Erforschung der Bibel (und hierbei gerade des Alten Testamentes) implementieren wollten, wurden bis ins 20. Jh. nur an Fakultäten der evangelischen Kirchen herangezogen, während von Seiten der katholischen Theologie anfangs große Ablehnung und dann ein schrittweises Nachholen verzeichnet wurde[249]. So ist gerade jene Tradition, welche die religiöse Autorität einzig auf die Schrift legt gerade aufgrund des göttlichen Ursprunges auch jene, welche die Methoden hervorbrachte, die biblischen Texte als weltliches Produkt entsprechend dekonstruieren. Diese Ambivalenz muss jedoch nicht als Widerspruch dastehen, sondern gerade die Agenda der *participatory revelation* zum Ausdruck bringen. Denn die Annahme, die darin steckt ist, dass es einen Moment göttlicher Offenbarung gibt, welche sich in der Gestalt menschlicher Wörter und den damit verbunden Ausdrucksformen, literarischen Gattungen und historisch-kontextuellen Bezügen zeigt. So stellen historisch-kritische Methoden gerade jene Werkzeuge dar, um die Offenbarung Gottes so wieder hervorzubringen, dass sie den HörerInnen von heute zugänglich wird. Um es mit *Dei Verbum* auszudrücken: „Da Gott in der Heiligen Schrift durch Menschen nach Menschenart gesprochen hat, muß

---

[246] vgl. Kapitel 4.3

[247] Miethke et al. 1980, 32 zitieren dabei die Schriften Luthers *Assertio omnium articulorum M. Lutheri per bullam Leonis X. novissimam damnatorum. (1520)* und *Iudicivm Martini Lutheri De Votis Monasticis (1521)*

[248] Fritz et al. 1980, 348

[249] Fritz et al. 1980, 354

der Schrifterklärer, um zu erfassen, was Gott uns mitteilen wollte, sorgfältig erforschen, was die heiligen Schriftsteller wirklich zu sagen beabsichtigten und was Gott mit ihren Worten kundtun wollte“ (DV 12).

Dennoch gibt es zahlreiche reformierte Traditionen, welche historisch-kritische Methoden ablehnen im Sinne der *sola scriptur,* da diese externen Einflüsse darstellen und etwa auf den Rationalismus setzen – „which claims that human reason is the means of establishing the meaning and the divine origin of the Bible“[250] – und für die Bibelinterpretation ganz auf schriftimmanente Auslegungszugänge setzen. Obgleich selbst das *sola scriptura* Verständnis stark nach Glaubensgemeinschaft variiert[251] und dieses Thema hier nicht zur Genüge ausdiskutiert werden kann, soll in dieser Diskussion ein Dilemma kurz angerissen werden, da es wesentlich mit den Implikationen dieser Arbeit zusammenhängt. Wenn wir Phänomene wie die innerbiblische Schriftauslegung oder die Pluralität der Kanonbildung betrachten, muss die Einheit und die Annahme von Schrift als Referenzgröße jenseits von historischen und kulturellen Kontextfaktoren sowie der Anbindung an eine gewisse Glaubensgemeinschaft stark in Frage gestellt werden. In anderen Worten: Man kann die Heilige Schrift(en) nicht ohne die Kenntnisse der Kontexte in der sie verfasst, redigiert und zu einem verbindlichen Kanon erstellt wurden (also eben Schrift-externe) so lesen, dass man den Anspruch erheben kann, zuverlässig über die Intention hinter dem Wort Gottes sprechen zu können. Folgen wir der These von Sommer, wo für das Judentum eine strenge Trennung zwischen Mündlicher und Schriftlicher Torah durch die Betrachtung der *participatory theory of revelation* fällt[252], muss zugleich überlegt werden, welche Analogien für das Christentum formuliert werden können. An dieser Stelle soll die These aufgeworfen werden, wie sola scriptura – im Sinne einer Fixierung auf eine Version des Textes mit einer überhöhten Verbindlichkeit und Selbstreferenzialität – bedeutet, dass mit einer gewissen Willkürlichkeit der Produktionsstrang der Verschriftlichung und Versprachlichung der göttlichen Offenbarung an einem bestimmten Zeitpunkt der Rezeptionsgeschichte unterbrochen wird. Die Frage nach den Kriterien dieser Selektion, die etwa in der Diskussion um die Kanonbildung gesucht werden, ist bei Religionsgemeinschaften, die eine strenge

[250] Santrac 2013, 116 zitiert dabei eine Position aus dem konservativen Evangelikalismus.

[251] Siehe Santrac 2013 für einen ersten Überblick.

[252] vgl. Abschnitt 5.3.3

sola scriptura vertreten, noch brisanter, da diese sich in einer Diskontinuität mit jenen Gemeinschaften verstehen, welche die Bildung des Kanons verantwortet haben.

Mit der Orientierung an *sola scriptura* findet sich meistens eine Präferenz für das Literalverständnis, die wiederum auf die Annahme zurück geht, dass die Worte der Heiligen Schrift deshalb verbindlich sind, da sie von Gott kommen. In der Terminologie von Sommer würde sich eine solche Auffassung unter *stenographic theory* einordnen lassen, wodurch sich ein spannender Diskussionspunkt im Anschluss an die dargestellten exegetischen Betrachtungen ergibt:

Im Vergleich des Verständnisses von direkter und indirekter Wiedergabe der Worte des Dekaloges fand Sommer für die vier Quellen der Pentateuch[253] einen besonders markanten Unterschied, der auf den ersten Blick paradox erscheinen mag. So stellt Deuteronomium (Dtn 5) jenes Dokument dar, welches die Worte der Offenbarung Gottes am Sinai als direkte Rede wiedergibt. Der Fokus wird in der Darstellung ganz auf verbale Aspekte gerichtet und das gesamte Volk konnte an der Offenbarung akustisch teilhaben. Die Priesterschrift hingegen liegt auf dem anderen Ende des Kontinuums und zeigt eine klares Verständnis einer indirekten Offenbarung, wo die Inhalte der Offenbarung Gottes über Propheten (Moses und Aaron) dem Volk weitergegeben wurden, die nicht nur den Dekalog umfassen, sondern auch die kultischen Gebote in den Büchern Levitikus (Lev 11-25;27) sowie Numeri (Num 35-36). In dieser Pentateuchquelle wird eher eine metaphorische Sprache bevorzugt, mit einem besonderen Augenmerk auf Inhalte der Offenbarung zu kultischen Partikularismen.

Der Punkt der hierbei paradox erscheinen mag, ist die Verknüpfung des Verständnisses mit der theologische Ausrichtung der Dokumente, denn es mag auf dem ersten Blick erwartungswidrig erscheinen, dass das Deuteronomium, das ein Bild einer solidarischen Gesellschaft entwirft, von einsichtigen Individuen, welche die Bedeutung der Gebote für das eigene Wohlergehen erkennen, zugleich auch jenes ist, welches ein solches stenographisches Verständnis vertritt. Die priesterliche Schrift, als jene Quelle der Kult- und Reinheitsgeboten, die aus der Außenperspektive die jüdische Glaubenspraxis als einengend und streng erscheinen lassen, vertritt hingegen ein

[253] vgl. die detaillierte Darstellung in Abschnitt 5.3.1

Verständnis von Geboten und Offenbarung, die durch die Partizipation von menschlichen Figuren mitgeformt wurden.

Kann, mit gebotener Vorsicht, ein Vergleich zum heutigen Schriftverständnis gezogen werden? Ich meine ja, denn die, in der Öffentlichkeit oft als repressiv verstandene Morallehre der katholischen Kirche, wird nicht direkt über die Worte der Heiligen Schrift abgeleitet, sondern ist lehramtlich formuliert worden in Anlehnung an die Heilige Schrift und über die Autorität unter Einwirkung des Heiligen Geistes. Evangelikale und freikirchliche Gemeinden hingegen werden von außen oft als stärker an der Autonomie und Freiheit der Gläubigen orientiert eingeschätzt, berufen sich für normative Fragen aber meist direkt auf die Worte der Heiligen Schrift und sehen eben nur diese als verbindlich an. Es stellt sich die Frage, welches Schriftverständnis und welche „theologische Architektur" den ontologisch korrekteren Zugang zur Auslegung der Offenbarung Gottes darstellen und in Folge dessen am fruchtbarsten ist, um – neben religiös-kultischen – vor allem sittlich-moralische Gebote und Orientierungsreferenzen hervorzubringen, welche den Gläubigen ein verantwortungsvolles Zusammenleben in der Gesellschaft eröffnen. Auf der Erfahrungsebene muss festgestellt werden, dass es sowohl für Gemeinschaften, die sich ganz an der Autorität der Heiligen Schrift orientieren, wie für jene, die sich stärker an der Auslegung und Mediation der Heiligen Schrift über religiöse Institutionen ausrichten, genauso viele positive wie negative Beispiele gibt. Man kann aus dem gelebten Schrift- und Autoritätsverständnis nicht direkt auf das Engagement im Einsatz zu Fragen der Menschenrechte, der Gleichbehandlung und gesellschaftlichen Inklusion schließen. Aber dennoch: Diese Arbeit soll aufgezeigt haben, dass dort, wo ein statisches Verständnis von Offenbarung und Schrift im Wege steht, das den göttlichen Ursprung der biblischen Worte schützen möchte, es dennoch möglich ist, den Text als Kulturprodukt zu behandeln ohne die transzendenten Dimension abzusprechen. Für jene Traditionen, welche Schrift und Tradition als Äquivalent denken, erwächst jedoch die Aufgabe, die menschliche Kontingenz der Formulierungen stets zu berücksichtigen, und auf jene Denkfiguren zu setzen – sei es die Auffassung im Judentum, in der bei der Offenbarung in Sinai, von der mündliche Torah bis hin zu den Fragen begabter Studierender, schon alles mitgegeben wurde[254],

[254] vgl. Abschnitt 5.3.3

oder die Wirkung des Heiligen Geistes in der Versammlung der Kirche[255] –, die im Vermächtnis der Göttlichen Offenbarung unter der Providenz Gottes für Innovation stehen.

7.3 Implikationen für theologische Forschung und Pastoral

Das Werk von Benjamin Sommer und die Möglichkeiten, die sich in einer Diplomarbeit ergeben, zeigen wie ertragreich die Verbindung aus exegetischen Betrachtungen, philosophischen Denkmodellen und theologiegeschichtlich-systematischen Referenzen sein kann. Dies führt uns auf die Forschungsausrichtung zurück wie Sommer sie für die *Dialogical Biblical Theology*[256] formuliert hatte, gerade auch für das Engagement für die Themen, welche von der Gesellschaft an jene, die Theologie treiben, herangebracht werden. Insbesondere fiel mir an vielen Stellen auf, wie es nicht nur für den biblischen Bereich von immanenter Bedeutung ist historisch-kritische Methoden anzuwenden, sondern eben auch für das Nachbiblische Schrifttum der Fall ist[257]. Für das katholische Lehramt ist es in entsprechender Weise interessant gewesen mit der dogmatischen Konstitution *Dei Verbum* ein Dokument zu haben, dass diskursiv behandelt worden ist, mit entsprechender Dokumentation über den Entstehungsprozess und die Referenzrahmen, welche in Folge dann über archivarische Arbeiten rekonstruiert und weiter kommentiert werden können[258]. Neben dem verstärkten Fokus auf kontextuell rekonstruktive Methoden in der theologischen Forschung, meine ich, soll sich die Theologie auch weiterhin im Dienste des Wort Gottes und in der Weitergabe der Offenbarung sehen, insofern sie die notwendigen Werkzeuge bereitstellt um das Tradierte gut aufzuarbeiten für den Verkündigungsdienst in den Gemeinden und in der Öffentlichkeit.

Drängt man in der theologischen Forschungspraxis mehr auf historisch-kritische Methoden, muss in der schulischen und pastoralen Praxis jedoch mit einer gewissen Desorientierung gerechnet werden. Aus dem Freundes- und Bekanntenkreis weiß ich, wie der Austausch über manche spannende Erkenntnisse aus der Exegese (etwa die womöglich nie stattgefunden Volkszählung zur Geburt Jesu) nicht nur stark

---

[255] vgl. Kapitel 6.2

[256] Sommer 2009

[257] Für einen Überblick zu Arbeiten zur rabbinischen Literatur siehe Gafni 2011

[258] vgl. Kapitel 6 und insbesondere die Arbeit von Kirchschläger 2014

verwirrend sein mögen, sondern von einem zuvor unreflektiertem Verständnis von biblischer Schrift, mit der Annahme eines womöglich göttlichen Ursprunges, die Position in eine Haltung umschlägt, die dieses Schriftstück eher als Betrug und Fälschung der Fakten versteht. Die Ambivalenz die Bibel als Spannungsfeld zwischen göttlicher Offenbarung und menschlicher Formulierung zu denken ist dabei eine Höchstleistung, die nicht einfach so vorausgesetzt werden kann. Dabei gilt es als Aufgabe für theologisch gebildete Menschen gerade in der Praxis die Unterstützungsleistung zu bieten, diese zwei Aspekte der Heiligen Schrift nicht als kontradiktorisch, sondern als komplementär zu vermitteln und gerade die darin immanente Botschaft „heraus zu kitzeln“: Was es bedeutet, wenn Gott Menschen zu MitverfasserInnen macht und die Schwäche und Begrenztheit des Wortes in der historischen Formulierung annimmt und gleichzeitig den Beistand zusichert, durch das Hören auf das Wort Gottes, im Forschen und Austauschen, die Botschaft in der Offenbarung zu erschließen.

8 Schlussbetrachtung

Diese Arbeit wurde für das Fach alttestamentliche Bibelwissenschaft geschrieben, wobei jedoch zu Beginn feststand, dass sie unter den Vorzeichen der Bibeltheologie verfasst wird, da sie sich methodisch und thematisch über die Grenzen der Arbeit mit alttestamentlichen Texten hinausbewegt. Es wurden viele Themenfelder angerissen: jüdisches Schrifttum und Philosophie, Exegese, bis hin zu Fragen, die eher in der systematischen Theologie behandelt werden. Aber gerade die Verbindung über die Grenzen eines Faches hinweg machen es möglich, grundlegende Fragen wie das Verständnis von Schrift differenziert anzugehen und dabei war es für mich besonders wichtig, dass die exegetischen Aspekte in der Diskussion des Begriffes der *participatory revelation* im Mittelpunkt stehen. Mit den Arbeiten von Benjamin Sommer meine ich eine gute Vorlage gefunden zu haben, der mehrere Disziplinen souverän vertreten und so eine fundierte Analyse bieten kann.

Besonders fruchtbar schien für mich die Möglichkeit, mich auf diese Fragestellung im Judentum zu vertiefen und zu vergleichen, wie Denkmodelle angewandt werden um zum Teil unterschiedliche, aber im Kern an gemeinsame Problematiken adressierte Fragen eine fundierte Antwort zu geben. Oft braucht es auch einen persönlichen Zugang, der manche Hemmschwellen sich mit einem sonst im Studium eher am Rande angesprochenes Thema auseinanderzusetzen zu überwinden hilft. Ganz wesentlich war für mich dabei die Möglichkeit, in Haifa ein Semester zu studieren und über die Vorbereitung eines Referates, in dem ich der Frage nachging, ob es ein Hierarchie zwischen der Torah und den anderen Schriften des Tenachs gibt, zu dieser Publikation von Benjamin Sommer zu kommen.

Angesprochen haben mich diese Publikation und die Möglichkeiten, die ich darin für eine Abschlussarbeit sah, auch deshalb, weil sie aktuelle Fragen behandeln, die von der Gesellschaft an die Religion gestellt werden. Die Frage, unter welchen Bedingungen biblische Schriften als Formulierung von sittlichen Normen herangezogen werden können und inwiefern es deren Eigenschaft gerecht wird, im Inhalt einen wörtlichen Ausdruck des Willen Gottes zu sehen, trifft für mich ganz wesentlich auf Anliegen, die eine Theologie im 21. Jh. verantworten muss. Von der ersten Lehrveranstaltung an habe ich an der theologischen Fakultät gelernt, wie Theologie nicht nur nach dem Sinn suchen muss, sondern sich auch die Frage nach der Bedeutung zu stellen hat. Sinn macht Theologie, wenn sie sich an methodologischen

Richtlinien der jeweiligen akademischen Disziplinen hält und die Forschungsfragen mit der nötigen Sorgfalt bearbeitet. Die Frage nach der Bedeutung hängt damit zusammen, welchen Einfluss der theologische Diskurs auf die Öffentlichkeit ausübt. Auch Theologie wird daran gemessen, ob sie einen Beitrag für eine gerechtere und inklusivere Gesellschaft leisten kann. Das habe ich in Salzburg gelernt.

9 Bibliographie

Baden, Joel S. 2012. *The Composition of the Pentateuch: Renewing the Documentary Hypothesis*, The Anchor Yale Bible reference library (New Haven: Yale University Press)

Bakhos, Carol (ed.). 2006. *Current Trends in the Study of Midrash*, Supplements to the Journal for the study of Judaism, 106 (Leiden: Brill)

Barr, James. 1999. *The Concept of Biblical Theology: An Old Testament Perspective* (Minneapolis: Fortress Press)

—— 2004. 'Unity: Whitin and After the Canon', in Christine Helmer and Christof Landmesser (eds), *One scripture or many?: Canon from Biblical, theological, and philosophical perspectives* (Oxford: Oxford Univ. Press), pp. 151–58

Barton, Assnat. 2011. 'Seeing the Thunder: Narrative Images of the Ten Commandments', in Henning Reventlow and Ya'îr Hôfman (eds), *The Decalogue in Jewish and Christian tradition,* T & T Clark library biblical studies, 509 (New York: T & T Clark), pp. 13–31

—— 2016. 'Legal Texts', in John Barton (ed.), *The Hebrew Bible: A critical companion* , pp. 160–81

Batnitzsky, Leora. 2006. 'Revelation and Neues Denken: Rethinking Buber and Rosenzweig on the Law', in Michael Zank (ed.), *New perspectives on Martin Buber: [conference "Martin Buber: Neue Perspektiven/New Perspectives", held on July 6 and 7, 2003, ... in Frankfurt],* Religion in philosophy and theology, 22 (Tübingen: Mohr Siebeck), pp. 149–64

Blum, Georg G. 1971. *Offenbarung und Überlieferung: Die dogmatische Konstitution Dei verbum des II. Vaticanums im Lichte altkirchlicher und moderner Theologie*, Forschung zur systematischen und ökumenischen Theologie, 28 (Göttingen: Vandenhoeck & Ruprecht)

Brecht, Bertolt. 2013. *Leben des Galilei: Schauspiel*, 71st edn, Edition Suhrkamp, 1 (Frankfurt am Main: Suhrkamp)

Brill, Alan. 2006. 'Aggadic Man: The Poetry and Rabbinic Thought of Abraham Joshua Heschel', *Meorot*, 6.1: 2–21

—— 2015. *Interview with Benjamin Sommer on Revelation and Authority: Sinai in Jewish Scripture and Tradition*, https://kavvanah.wordpress.com/2015/05/13/interview-with-benjamin-sommer-on-revelation-and-authority-sinai-in-jewish-scripture-and-tradition/ (accessed 22 April 2018)

Buber, Martin. 1968. *On the Bible: Eighteen Studies* (New York: Schocken Books)

—— 1973. *Das dialogische Prinzip* (Heidelberg: Lamberg Schneider)

Collins, John J. 2004. *Introduction to the Hebrew Bible: [with CD-ROM]* (Minneapolis, Minn.: Fortress Press)

Commentary Magazine. 1966. *The State of Jewish Belief*, https://www.commentarymagazine.com/articles/the-state-of-jewish-belief/ (accessed 15 April 2018)

Dozeman, Thomas B. 1989. *God on the Mountain: A Study of Redaction, Theology, and Canon in Exodus 19-24*, Monograph series / Society of Biblical Literature, 37 (Atlanta, Ga.: Scholars Press)

Editors of Commentary Magazine. 1966. 'The State of Jewish Belief', *Commentary*, 1 August

Eichrodt, Walther. 1961. *Theology of the Old Testament*, The Old Testament library (Philadelphia, Pennsylvania: Westminster Press)

Encyclopaedia Judaica. 1971a. *Gemara*, http://judaism_enc.enacademic.com/7052 (accessed 7 February 2018)

—— 1971b. *Midrash Ha-Gadol*, http://judaism_enc.enacademic.com/13602/MIDRASH_HA-GADOL (accessed 7 February 2018)

—— 2007. *Soferim*, http://www.jewishvirtuallibrary.org/soferim (accessed 7 February 2018)

Farber, Seth. 2018. *Don't let Israel's ignorant, politicized rabbinate bully Jews abroad: Haaretz.com*, https://www.haaretz.com/opinion/.premium-don-t-let-israel-s-ignorant-politicized-rabbinate-bully-jews-abroad-1.6181395 (accessed 24 June 2018)

Fleischacker, Samuel. 2014. *Making Sense of the Revelation at Sinai: Revisiting Maimonides' Account of Revelation*, https://thetorah.com/making-sense-of-the-revelation-at-sinai/ (accessed 15 April 2018)

Fraade, Steven D. 2012. 'Concepts of Scripture in Rabbinic Judaism: Oral Torah and Written Torah', in Benjamin D. Sommer (ed.), *Jewish concepts of Scripture: A comparative introduction* (New York, NY: New York Univ. Press), pp. 31–46

Friedmann, Shamma, and Leib Moscovitz. 1997. 'Talmud', in Geoffrey Wigoder and R. J. Z. Werblowsky (eds), *The Oxford dictionary of the Jewish religion* (New York: Oxford University Press), pp. 668–72

Fritz, Volkmar et al. 1980. 'Bibelwissenschaft', in Gerhard Krause and Gerhard Müller (eds), *Theologische Realenzyklopädie* (Berlin, New York: de Gruyter), pp. 316–409

Gafni, Isaiah. 2011. 'Rethinking Talmudic History: The challenge of literary and redaction criticism', *Jewish History*, 25.3/4: 355–75

Gerdmar, Anders. 2009. *Roots of theological anti-Semitism: German biblical interpretation and the Jews, from Herder and Semler to Kittel and Bultmann*, Studies in Jewish history and culture, 20 (Leiden u.a.: Brill)

Golnik, David. 2013. *Why the State of Israel Should Abolish the Chief Rabbinate: The Schechter Institutes*, https://www.schechter.edu/why-the-state-of-israel-should-abolish-the-chief-rabbinate/ (accessed 24 June 2018)

Graham, William. 1987. 'Scripture', in Mircea Eliade and Charles Adams (eds), *Encyclopedia of Religion* (New York: Macmillan), pp. 133–45

Greenspahn, Frederick E. 2007. 'Jewish Ambivalence Towards the Bible', *Hebrew Studies*, 48: 7–21

Harhowitz, Rivka. 1989. 'Revelation in the Bible according to Twentieth-Century Jewish Philsophy', in Arthur Green (ed.), *Jewish spirituality: From Sixteenth-Century Revival to the Present,* World spirituality, 14 (New York: Crossroad Publ. Comp), pp. 346–70

Heschel, Abraham J. 1951. *Man Is Not Alone: A Philophy of Religion* (New York: Farrar Straus and Giroux)

—— 1956. *God in search of man: a philosophy of Judaism* (Philadelphia, Pa.: Jewish Publication Society)

Holtz, Barry W. 2011. 'Bible: Teaching the Bible in Our Times', in Helena Miller, Lisa Grant and Alex Pomson (eds), *International Handbook of Jewish Education,* International Handbooks of Religion and Education (Dordrecht: Springer Netherlands), pp. 373–88

International Committee on English in the Liturgy. 2010. 'The Roman Missal'

Jewish Encyclopedia. *Talmud*, http://www.jewishencyclopedia.com/articles/11869-palestinian-talmud (accessed 6 February 2018)

Katz, Steven T. 1978. 'Dialogue and Revelation in the Thought of Martin Buber', *Religious Studies*, 14.1: 57–68

Kent, Orit, and Allison Cook. 2014. 'Teachers As Learners and Practitioners: Shifting Teaching Practice through Havruta Pedagogy', *Religious Education*, 109.5: 507–25

Kirchschläger, Walter. 1985. *Dogmatische Konstitution Über die göttliche Offenbarung: "Dei verbum" ; vollst. Text ; Einführung und Kurzkommentar* (Klosterneuburg: Verl. Österreichisches Kath. Bibelwerk)

—— 2014. *Ob die Bibel irren kann?: Das Gottesprojekt Bibel*, Kardinal-König-Bibliothek, 5 (Wien, Graz, Klagenfurt: Verl.-Gruppe Styria)

Kratz, Reinhard. 2011. 'The Pentateuch in Current Research: Consensus and Debate', in Thomas B. Dozeman, Konrad Schmid and Baruch Schwarz (eds), *The Pentateuch: International perspectives on current research,* Forschungen zum Alten Testament, 78 (Tübingen: Mohr Siebeck), pp. 31–62

Lehman, Marjorie, and Jane Kanarek. 2011. 'Talmud: Making a Case for Talmud Pedagogy—The Talmud as an Educational Model', in Helena Miller, Lisa Grant and Alex Pomson (eds), *International Handbook of Jewish Education,* International Handbooks of Religion and Education (Dordrecht: Springer Netherlands), pp. 581–96

Levenson, John D. 1987. 'Why Jews are Not Interested in Biblical Theology', in Jacob Neusner (ed.), *Judaic perspectives on ancient Israel* (Philadelphia: Fortress Pr), pp. 281–307

Lim, Timothy H. 2010. 'The Defilement Of The Hands As A Principle Determining The Holiness Of Scriptures', *The Journal of Theological Studies*, 61.2: 501–15

—— 2013. *The Formation of the Jewish Canon* (New Haven: Yale University Press)

Meade, David G. 1986. *Pseudonymity and canon: An investigation into the relationship of authorship and authority in Jewish and earliest Christian tradition* (Grand Rapids, Mich.: Eerdmans)

Merk, Otto. 1980. 'Biblische Theologie', in Gerhard Krause and Gerhard Müller (eds), *Theologische Realenzyklopädie* (Berlin, New York: de Gruyter), pp. 426–77

Metzger, Bruce M. 1997. *The Canon of the New Testament: Its Origin, Development, and Significance* (Oxford: Clarendon Press)

Miethke, Jürgen et al. 1980. 'Autorität', in Gerhard Krause and Gerhard Müller (eds), *Theologische Realenzyklopädie* (Berlin, New York: de Gruyter), pp. 17–51

Mirvis, Ephraim. 2012. *Two heads are better for learning than one: Children in the general school system could gain from traditional methods of studying Torah*, https://www.thejc.com/judaism/features/two-heads-are-better-for-learning-than-one-1.33315 (accessed 24 June 2018)

Morenz, Siegfried. 1950. 'Entstehung und Wesen der Buchreligion', *Theologischen Literaturzeitung*: 709–16

myjewishlearning.com. 2018. *Leviticus*, https://www.myjewishlearning.com/article/leviticus/ (accessed 10 February 2018)

Najman, Hindy. 2003. *Seconding Sinai: The Development of Mosaic Discourse in Second Temple Judaism*, Supplements to the Journal for the study of Judaism, v. 77 (Leiden, Boston: Brill)

Neusner, Jacob. 1982. 'Scripture and Mishnah: Authority and Selectivity', in Frederick E. Greenspahn (ed.), *Scripture in the Jewish and Christian traditions: Authority, interpretation, relevance* (Nashville: Abingdon), pp. 64–86

—— 2001. *The Theology of the Halakhah*, Brill reference library of ancient Judaism, v. 6 (Leiden, Boston, MA: Brill)

—— 2002. *How the Talmud Works*, The Brill reference library of ancient Judaism, v. 9 (Leiden, Boston: Brill)

—— 2005. 'Mishnah and the Oral Torah: What Did the Rabbinic Sages Mean by "the Oral Torah"?', in Jacob Neusner, Alan J. Avery-Peck and William S. Green (eds), *The Eencyclopaedia of Judaism*, 2nd edn (Leiden: Brill), pp. 1707–16

Noth, Martin. 1962. *Exodus: A commentary* (Westminster Press)

Oswald, Wolfgang. 2014. 'Lawgiving at the Mountain of God: (Exodus 19-24)', in Thomas B. Dozeman, Craig A. Evans and Joel N. Lohr (eds), *The Book of Exodus: Composition, Reception, and Interpretation,* Supplements to Vetus Testamentum, 164 (Leiden: Brill), pp. 169–92

Papst Johannes Paul II. 1992. *Ansprache an die Teilnehmer der Vollversammlung der Päpstlichen Akademie der Wissenschaften: vom 31. Oktober 1992*, https://w2.vatican.va/content/john-paul-ii/de/speeches/1992/october/documents/hf_jp-ii_spe_19921031_accademia-scienze.html (accessed 26 June 2018)

Pius XI. 1937. *Enzyklika Mit brennender Sorge*, http://w2.vatican.va/content/pius-xi/de/encyclicals/documents/hf_p-xi_enc_14031937_mit-brennender-sorge.html (accessed 21 June 2018)

Plaskow, Judith. 1990. *Standing again at Sinai: Judaism from a feminist perspective* (New York, NY: Harper & Row)

—— 2008. 'Contemporary Reflection, Vayeira', *The Torah: A Women's Commentary*: 107–08

Pollock, Benjamin. 2014. *Franz Rosenzweig's Conversions: World Denial and World Redemption* (Bloomington: Indiana University Press)

—— 2015. *Franz Rosenzweig: The Stanford Encyclopedia of Philosophy*, https://plato.stanford.edu/archives/sum2015/entries/rosenzweig/ (accessed 5 March 2018)

Potok, Chaim. 1965. *Principles of the Jewish Faith, by Louis Jacobs*, https://www.commentarymagazine.com/articles/principles-of-the-jewish-faith-by-louis-jacobs/ (accessed 15 April 2018)

Rahner, Karl, and Herbert Vorgrimler. 1990. *Kleines Konzilskompendium: Sämtliche Texte des Zweiten Vatikanums ; allgemeine Einleitung - 16 spezielle Einführungen - ausführliches Sachregister ; mit einem Nachtrag vom Oktober 1968: Die nachkonziliare Arbeit der römischen Kirchenleitung*, 22nd edn, Herderbücherei, 270 (Freiburg im Breisgau: Herder)

Rosenzweig, Franz. 1921. *Der Stern der Erlösung* (Frankfurt a.M.: Kaufmann)

Rosenzweig, Franz, and Nahum N. Glatzer. 1961. *Franz Rosenzweig: His Life and Thought*, 3rd edn (Indianapolis: Hackett)

Rothschild, Fritz A., and Ephraim Meir. 2007. 'Heschel, Abraham Joshua', in Michael Berenbaum and Fred Skolnik (eds), *Encyclopaedia Judaica*, 2nd edn (Detroit: Macmillan Reference USA), pp. 70–72

Rutishauser, Christian M. 2016. *Christlichen Glauben denken Wien: Im Dialog mit der jüdischen Tradition*, Forum Christen und Juden, Band 15 (LIT Verlag)

Santrac, Aleksandar S. 2013. 'The Sola Scriptura Principle in the Current Debate', *Journal of the Adventist Theological Society*, 24.1: 107–26

Schwarz, Baruch. 1997. 'What really happened at Mount Sinai?', *Bible Review*, 46: 21–46

Seltzer, Robert M. 1980. *Abraham Joshua Heschel: A Prophet's Prophet*, https://www.myjewishlearning.com/article/abraham-joshua-heschel-a-prophets-prophet/ (accessed 15 April 2018)

Silverman, Jason M. 2011. 'Pseudepigraphy, Anonymity, and Auteur Theory', *Religion and the Arts*, 15.4: 520–55

Simon, U. 1999. 'The Place Of The Bible In Israeli Society: From National Midrash To Existential Peshat', *Modern Judaism*, 19.3: 217–39

Sommer, Benjamin D. 2004. 'Unity and Plurality in Jewish Canons: The Case of the Oral and Written Torahs', in Christine Helmer and Christof Landmesser (eds), *One scripture or many?: Canon from Biblical, theological, and philosophical perspectives* (Oxford: Oxford Univ. Press), pp. 108–50

—— 2009. 'Dialogical Biblical Theology: A Jewish Approach to Reading Scripture Theologically', in Leo G. Perdue, Robert Morgan and Benjamin D. Sommer (eds), *Biblical theology: Introducing the conversation,* The library of biblical theology (Nashville: Abingdon Press)

—— 2015. *Revelation and Authority: Sinai in Jewish Scripture and Tradition*, The Anchor Yale Bible reference library (New Haven and London: Yale University Press)

—— 2017. *A Symposium: Revelation and Authority: Author's Response*, https://thetorah.com/revelation-and-authority/authors-response/ (accessed 22 April 2018)

Sprinkle, Joe M. 2004. 'Law And Narrative in Exodus 19-24', *JETS*, 47.2: 235–52

Stemberger, Günter. 1992. *Einleitung in Talmud und Midrasch*, 8th edn, Beck-Studium (München: Beck)

Stowasser, Martin. 2016. *Vaticanum, Zweites: in: WiBiLex*, https://www.bibelwissenschaft.de/stichwort/25750/ (accessed 14 February 2018)

Sweeney, Marvin A. 2008. 'Jewish Biblical Theology', in Frederick E. Greenspahn (ed.), *The Hebrew Bible: New insights and scholarship,* Jewish studies in the 21st century , pp. 191–208

—— 2012. *Tanak: A theological and critical introduction to the Jewish Bible* (Minneapolis: Fortress Press)

—— 2016. 'Jewish Biblical Theology: An Ongoing Dialogue', *Interpretation: A Journal of Bible and Theology*, 70.3: 314–25

The Old Testament in Greek. 1906/2010. 'ΕΞΟΔΟΣ', in Alan E. Brooke (ed.), *The Old Testament in Greek: According to the Text of Codex Vaticanus, Supplemented from Other Uncial Manuscripts, with a Critical Apparatus Containing the Variants of the Chief Ancient Authorities for the Text of the Septuagint,* Cambridge library collection. Religion (Cambridge: publisher not identified), pp. 155–293

van der Toorn, Karel. 2009. *Scribal Culture and the Making of the Hebrew Bible* (Cambridge: Harvard University Press)

Walfish, Avraham. 1997a. 'Mishnah', in Geoffrey Wigoder and R. J. Z. Werblowsky (eds), *The Oxford dictionary of the Jewish religion* (New York: Oxford University Press), pp. 471–72

—— 1997b. 'Tosefta', in Geoffrey Wigoder and R. J. Z. Werblowsky (eds), *The Oxford dictionary of the Jewish religion* (New York: Oxford University Press), pp. 699–700

Wigoder, Geoffrey, Fred Skolnik, and Shmuel Himelstein (eds). 2002. *The New Encyclopedia of Judaism* (New York, NY: New York Univ. Press)

Wigoder, Geoffrey, and R. J. Z. Werblowsky (eds). 1997. *The Oxford Dictionary of the Jewish Religion* (New York: Oxford University Press)

Zank, Michael, and Zachary Braiterman. 2014. *Martin Buber: The Stanford Encyclopedia of Philosophy*, https://plato.stanford.edu/archives/win2014/entries/buber/ (accessed 8 March 2018)

Zenger, Erich. 2008. *Einleitung in das Alte Testament*, 7th edn, Kohlhammer-Studienbücher Theologie (Stuttgart: Kohlhammer)

Zweites Vatikanisches Konzil. 1965. *Dogmatische Konstitution DEI VERBUM: Über die göttliche Offenbarung*, http://www.vatican.va/archive/hist_councils/ii_vatican_council/documents/vat-ii_const_19651118_dei-verbum_ge.html (accessed 20 June 2018)

Printed by Books on Demand GmbH, Norderstedt / Germany